THE STRÖM TOYS

A PERPETUAL WISH BOOK

By Janet A. Strombeck
and
Richard H. Strombeck

Illustrated by Marlene Ekman

This book is dedicated to our children, whose help and judgments were invaluable, to their children who were pure inspiration, and to children of all ages everywhere.

Toy designs: The Ströms

Designer and editor: Ann Tomasic

Photography: Don Sala Photography

Published by: Rexstrom Company, Inc.
                    Sun Designs
                    P.O. Box 206
                    Delafield, WI 53018
                    Tel. 414-567-4255

Distributed by: Sterling Publishing Co.

ISBN #0-912355-01-8

Printed in the U.S.A.

FOREWORD

Following our tradition of publishing designs and plans for things that are unusual and hard to find, we have put together this extraordinary collection of wooden toys. I'm sure many of you already know our affection for wood and the many fine products and pleasures that come from it. Wooden toys are no exception.

In an earlier time, well-designed wooden toys were built by a father or grandfather and traditionally passed down to succeeding generations. These having survived, are now cherished family heirlooms. Broken parts were repaired or replaced and the toys lasted through years of play and use.

Today's high impact, injection molded toys are long-lived also even though programmed for early obsolescence. But, once they begin to crack, split, melt or warp, they are for all practical purposes irrecoverable.

It has been our opinion that many people prefer wooden toys for their children, and in

fact would take the time to build them if the toy design and function were to their liking. Interest in wooden toy construction by home craftsmen is growing. Witness to this fact is the large number of wooden toy books now on the market. Most of these books supply instruction for relatively quick toy projects, taking three to four hours maximum.

We believe the toy designs in this book are different from what is available elsewhere. The reason for this, of course, is that they were designed by the Ströms as told in the illustrated story that follows. All have been built in our home workshop; all are of *simple* construction. They do require more than three or four hours. *Not* because they are more complicated, but because they have more detail and finishing.

Many of the toys in this book can be completed with only hand tools. We used both hand and power tools. The principal power tools we used are a radial arm saw, sabre saw, jig saw, small belt sander and a small drill press. A small $89.00 wood lathe was used to make the wooden wagon wheels, lighthouse, and the round body of the *Norse Steed* rocking horse. I mention this only to encourage *all of you,* young and old, men and women, to try a toy project. *Everyone* can do it, and you already have plans right here to start with.

Most of the toys are made from fir, and a good number of them from just fir scraps, but hardwood can be used and is recommended for some toys such as the wagon and the buckets on the sand conveyor.

IMPORTANT! PLEASE READ

Even though we live on a lake and have a sand beach in our front yard, we know that weather and supervision requirements of young children limit their time outside, especially by water. Consequently, we have intended most of these toys to be what I call "rug" toys. When they are being "worked" indoors in place of sand, large navy beans, for example, can be used in the sand conveyor.

Complete construction plans are available for *all* wooden toys shown. If a toy has a part or parts that we feel are not readily available at a local source, we have included these parts with the plan package (for example, the brass drive chain, gears, and springs for the sand conveyor). Other parts are available from your local stores, such as rubber tread for the wooden wheels. If you cannot make a particular part, call us. The SUN DESIGNS number is 414-567-4255.

Good luck with your projects, and we'd be delighted to see a picture of your finished product. We sincerely hope that your children or grandchildren will have as much enjoyment from your efforts as ours have had.

THE STORY OF THE STRÖM TOYS

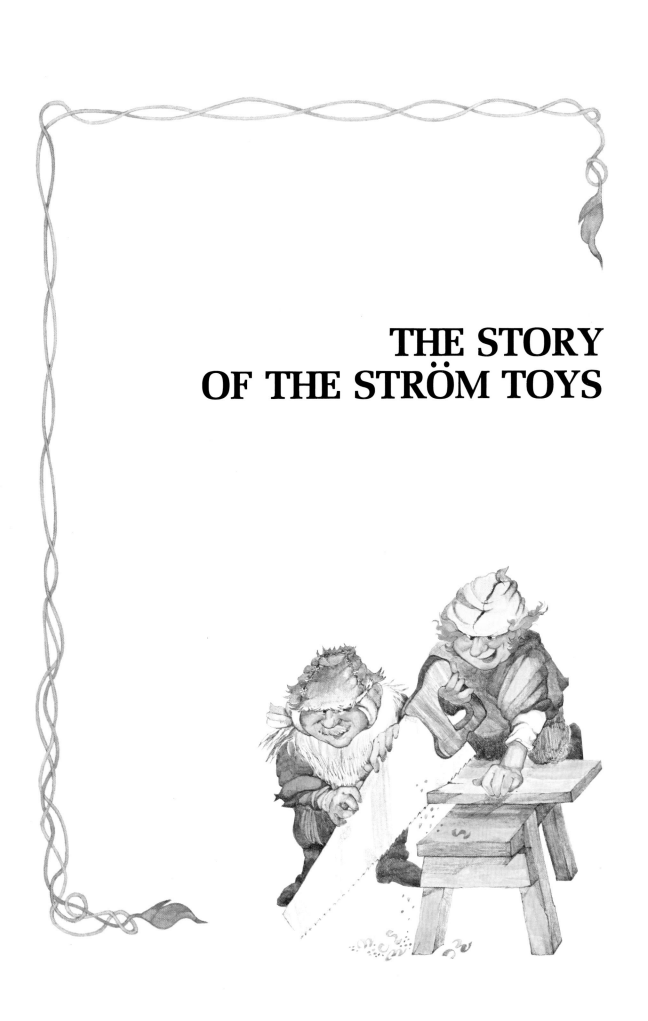

I have a strange story to tell.
You may not believe it,
but it really happened.

My story begins in December, a few weeks before Christmas. I was in my workshop trying to make toys for our eight grandchildren's Christmas party. Over and over again, I tried to create toys that would be special. But after many hours of work, all I had to show was a large pile of sawdust and a box of wood scraps. Tired and unhappy, I carried the box to the stove. I fed the wood scraps to the fire, piece by piece, each one reminding me of my failures. When the small iron stove was rumbling with heat, I sat down next to it on a low wooden chair, rested my head in my hands and stared out the window. Looking out across the unfrozen lake, I wondered how I could keep my promise to finish these toys. The warmth of the stove soon made me very drowsy. I took off my glasses, leaned back in my chair and before long I was asleep.

I can't tell you how long I slept before a sharp noise caused me to jump. Without my glasses and with sleepy eyes, I couldn't believe what I saw. Some very small people were laughing and pointing at me while I hunted for my glasses and rubbed my eyes. I must have been quite a sight. I put my glasses on and they were still there—standing everywhere and laughing at my surprise.

"This can't be," I muttered taking off my glasses. I rubbed my eyes again. I leaned over and touched the hot stove to see if I was dreaming. My finger blistered, and I knew I was wide awake.

Questions began to rush from my mouth faster than any person could answer them. And again, there were howls of laughter. As I was making a fool of myself, I sat down and began my questions in a slow, gentle way.

One of them called Stig, a kindly man with long, gray hair and bushy eyebrows arched over the bluest eyes, answered for everyone. As he spoke, the fine white hairs of his large mustache flew in all directions. He told me that they would like to return a favor. (I didn't know I had done one for them.) Stig went on to explain that they would build toys for me from the materials I already had in my workshop. They would use the plans they had once used for their children's toys.

"The time is short," Stig said. "It would be best to stop the questions so I can get everyone working. Then, I promise to answer more of your questions."

The questions were now popping into my mind so fast I would never remember them all. While they gathered around him to receive their orders, I saw that each one had his own special talent and each was very different from the other. In the middle of this group I saw a small, pesty duck. They called her Lena. She was squawking loudly, flapping her wings wildly and pecking at their shoes for attention. Way over on the other side of the shop, keeping away from Lena as much as possible, was a skunk called Max. He was very busy climbing over all the tools and inspecting every nook and cranny. I was fascinated by all of this. I also was anxious for them to get started so I could talk to Stig.

When Stig finished explaining the work at hand, they rushed in all different directions like a well-trained troupe of dancers. Soon, I saw strange things happening. There were two people working the saw, two men using a hammer, three of them passing boards back and forth, and two of them working the plane while the smallest one rode on it. The women with sandpaper on their feet, skated back and forth to the rhythm of the songs they sang.

As I watched Stig climbing up on the bench leg to finish our talk, I thought about touching the stove again to make sure I was really awake. Stig made himself comfortable on the bench and I quickly began asking my questions. The first one, of course, was who are you? Many more questions came and I soon forgot all about the time.

Much later I felt a hand on my shoulder and heard Janet, my wife, saying, "Dick, Dick, wake up. It's very late. I finished my baking and still you weren't in. So, I've come looking for you and here you are asleep. I see there's a lot of work done. You *must* be tired!

"But, I didn't do any of this," I said. "There were little people here. They were no more than eighteen inches tall and did all this work."

"Eighteen inches tall?" Janet said. "You must have been dreaming. Come to bed and we'll talk about it tomorrow."

The next morning, as we sat at the breakfast table, I began to tell Janet what I thought I remembered. But I must say, in the bright light of day I was not sure what *did* happen the night before. Janet patiently listened while I told her about the little people who call themselves Ströms.

"I remember Stig saying that they live on the other side of the lake, by the mouth of the stream. This is why they are called Ströms. It means *stream* in their language. They live in

their own well-hidden place, where the woods, stream and lake all meet. They have lived there for many years. They prefer to live far from big people who used to make fun of them and treat them badly.

"Their cozy little houses are made of branches, leaves and clay. They gather food from the forest—nuts, berries, fruits, maple syrup and root plants. They catch fish in the lake and stream. They make medicines from wild herbs and soap from wood ashes. Clothes are woven from fur that is shed by animals in the spring and are colored from plants found in the forest.

"So you see, they have
everything they need and are
free from the big people's
world. For fun, the Ströms sing
and dance to their own music,
and run and play with creatures
in the forest. In the fall, when

the food has been gathered, the storerooms are full, the snow begins to fall in the woods, they begin to do what they like better than anything else—to make the most wonderful wooden toys for their children.''

At this point, Janet leaned forward and said, "The toys made last night are different from anything I've seen before. I think they are beautiful, but I find it hard to believe this strange story of little people. Dick, if they were here, why didn't our dog, Nasha, bark? If they live in the woods, how do these eighteen-inch tall people get through snow that is three feet deep? Why have they come now when we've never seen them before? Why haven't others seen them?"

I shrugged and said, "I don't know. I can't answer any of these questions. Stig might have told me, but I can't remember. I must say, I'm not sure of anything this morning. If they were really here last night, they'll return to finish what they have started. If they don't come back, then I'll believe it was all a dream."

That seemed to end the questions for the moment. Janet walked to her office and I went to my workshop. First, I set aside the toys started last night not knowing how to continue. Then, I tidied up the workshop and began measuring wood for a new toy. I was all thumbs. I worried I would never finish anything. If the Ströms were a dream, I was in terrible trouble with my promised Christmas toys. I often looked out the window to see if any Ströms were coming.

I was growing more and more anxious as the sun started to set. I realized with a jolt that I had even forgotten to eat lunch in my worry and hurry. I rushed to join Janet in the kitchen for supper.

Later, I asked Janet to come out and help me work on the toys. As we walked through the fresh, new snow sparkling in the light of the full moon, we talked about how soon Christmas would be here.

"Maybe I shouldn't have promised the toys," I said sadly.

We entered the workshop, turned on the light, and the Ströms were waiting for us. I was greatly relieved and Janet sood stunned down to her boots.

"It can't be! I see it, but I can't believe it. How wonderful!" Janet kneeled down to a cheerful, doll-faced Ström. "What's your name? What are you holding?" Janet asked.

"My name is Ingrid," the little Ström replied. Ingrid held up a ball of fur close to her face. "And, this is my friend, Fritz. He's a baby raccoon."

Stig spoke up quickly, "If we are to finish some of the toys tonight, we must get to work right away. Everyone understands what has to be done. Tonight, we will use Dick to help move the larger pieces. And . . ."

Before Stig could say another word, Janet burst out with a volley of questions. As the others started to work, Stig stood with his chin thrust forward and rocking on his feet, muttering under his breath, "Questions, questions, always questions."

Looking up at Janet through his bushy eyebrows, he said, "Why can't big people believe in us without questions? We believe in them without questions. Why must you question a gift? Why can't you take our help as a sign of friendship? But to please you," he said with a sigh and without giving her a chance to answer, "I'll tell you why we are here."

He sat himself on the window ledge near Janet and started to explain.

"We are Ströms. We live by the water, and travel by water in boats we build ourselves. Sometimes people see us, but like you, they find it hard to believe. This morning, did Dick still believe that he saw us last night? And did he call his friends and say, 'I must tell you about the Ströms, people the size of my shoe who are working with me?'

"I think not," Stig said, "for if he had, they would say, 'Something is wrong with poor Dick.' Like everyone else, he tells no one about us. *That's* why you have never heard of us before."

Janet interrupted him and asked, "But why are you here making toys for us?"

"Do you remember how bad our winter was last year?"

"Oh, yes," Janet recalled. "The snow and ice were so thick. Many of the fish in the laked died and all of the forest animals had a very hard time finding food."

"Exactly," Stig said, pleased that she remembered and understood the problems. "You know, many years ago we had our troubles with big people who commanded us 'Do this, do that. Get this, get that. Clean this, clean that.' Never saying please or thank you. Now we have another problem and that is the Slug Hog. He's a mean, wicked, bad-smelling, ugly animal with a terrible temper and a huge appetite. This terrible beast frightens all who see him."

Stig's voice grew louder and started to tremble with rage.

"His runny, fiery eyes bug out of his huge head which is covered with lumps. His horns curl upward from his mouth past an ugly flat nose. His body, too, is covered with bumps down to his horrible big square feet. He comes crashing through the forest, ripping and destroying everything in his way. Just touching him makes animals sick. His breath makes bark pop off trees, chipmunks go crazy, and chickens fly backwards!

"Last year," Stig continued, "this demon beast came where we live, roaring and smashing everything in his way. He was looking for our food and found it. He destroyed our storerooms where all our winter food was kept. We were lucky to escape with our lives. We only did so by racing to our boats a few steps ahead of him. As we sailed off from shore, we heard him roaring on the beach. It was several days before we felt it was safe to go back. What a sad sight awaited us. Everything, and I mean *everything*, was destroyed. All the food had been eaten. But the ugly Slug Hog was gone."

Stig stood up, tucked his hands in his pockets and looked sadly across the workshop.

"Thankful as we were to be alive, we knew we were still in trouble. We had no home and, more importantly, no food. Ice, snow and broken branches were the only materials we found to build a home. We built it quickly to protect us from the weather. After finishing our ice house, we knew that we must find food soon or we would die. Everyone had to go and search for food. Only Ingrid would stay with the children. Oskar, who is our fortune teller and stargazer, made a map with places marked where to search, for each person.

"After studying and talking to the stars, Oskar sang out confidently:

> *The stars above have said to me:*
> *Great amounts of food there'll be*
> *And Max will be the one to find*
> *Bread and grains of every kind.*

"Then," Stig continued, "we made skis and snowshoes from the bark of trees for traveling over the high snow. We made sure Ingrid and the children were safe and we agreed to return in two days time. Everyone set forth on their way, each wishing the other good luck.

"Amanda and I traveled north. Klaus
and Helga crossed the lake to the west.
Olaf and Sofia hunted across the stream
to the east. Oskar and Frieda went south.
Johan and Mia fished on the shores
of the three lakes. All the
rest searched the forest.

"On the evening of the second day, a disappointed Oskar and Frieda decided to return home. Frieda, weary and hungry, could barely pull the basket with Max, the skunk, in it. All of a sudden Max bounded out of the basket and went running and leaping past them. In wonder, they ran after him. And there was your house and all the food you had set out for the animals. Oskar was so excited he began jumping up and down, yelling to Frieda:

The stars did say
We'd find a treasure,
On this day
And in good measure.
Now no fear
Thanks to Max!
One great cheer
For our full sacks.

"Anxious to return home with the food they had found," Stig went on, "they took the shortest way across the lake. They came home late in the evening. Everyone else had already returned empty-handed. We were a tired, sad and frightened group until Oskar, Frieda and Max showed their treasure. They told us more food was still there. Suddenly, there was joy and hope in the little ice house.

"We know there was no time to waste. No time to rest. Everyone knew another winter storm was on its way. We quickly made a large sleigh and harness and ten of us took pulling positions in the harness. The dark storm clouds were now covering the moon and we were soon in a fast run across the frozen lake with the sleigh following easily behind. Just as we arrived at the feeding station, the snow began to fall. Even though we had the

sleigh full in a very short time, the large
flakes were piling up very fast. It was
impossible for us to pull the heavy sleigh
through the deep, wet snow. Nasha had
been watching us from her dog house,
and since all animals are our friends
(except the smelly Slug Hog) we knew
that she would help. It would be no
problem for her to pull our sleigh across
the lake since she was a strong, fast
Siberian Husky.

"Connecting Nasha to the harness, four of us climbed onto the sleigh with the food, and others climbed onto Nasha's back. The good dog, with her great strength, lunged forward in a fast run into the blinding snowstorm. It was almost daylight when we arrived at our ice house, unloaded the food, collapsed inside the house too tired to even eat.

"When we awoke later that day, Nasha was gone. The storm was still blowing outside and lasted three more days.

"When the storm ended, five of us and Ingrid set out. We were met by Nasha romping through the know at the feeding station. To our surprise, it had been filled again with great amounts of seeds, grain and bread. Ingrid and Nasha met for the first time and quickly became friends. While the five of us were loading the sleigh, Nasha, with Ingrid screaming in delight on her back, ran like the wind between and around the trees. Finally, missing a turn, both tumbled into a big snowbank and disappeared. After a few minutes of silence, the snowbank began to shake and move. First, a bewildered Nasha poked her head through the snow. Suddenly, right next to her, the snow exploded and Ingrid popped out, laughing as hard as she could. Ingrid wished to play and told Nasha to hurry and get free of the snow so they could run some more.

"With the sleigh full once again and Nasha in harness with Ingrid riding like a jockey on her back, we made five trips back and forth. Each time the food and been refilled and each time Ingrid rode her make-believe 'horse' Nasha, in races through the woods.

"So, you see," Stig said quietly, "it was because of your help that we lived through the winter. We have rebuilt everything that was destroyed. We are ready now for the wicked Slug Hog if he ever returns."

With a look of surprise and a good feeling in her heart, Janet said, "So, that's why the food disappeared so quickly. I'm happy it was put to such good use. I also understand now why Nasha didn't bark last night, and I promise you, Stig, no more dumb questions."

Janet had been so interested in Stig's story she hadn't realized it was late and everyone had finished what they had started. As she looked at the work that was done, she told everyone how happy she was, how extraordinary the toys were and how thankful she was.

"Before anyone leaves, we will have hot chocolate and the cake that I baked," she said.

After finishing the refreshments, Stig thanked Janet and said they would return the following night to complete all the toys. The excitement of the evening and the happiness in knowing that Christmas would be as planned kept both Janet and I from sleeping. As we lay back on our pillows, smiles came on our faces as we recalled Stig or little Ingrid. The little Ström animals like Max, the skunk, or Lena, the duck, or Fritz, the baby raccoon, marched across our memories of this strange evening.

"Remember little bossy Amanda," I said aloud, "who always struts around like a tough general making sure each toy is perfect."

Janet laughed when I told her that Klaus said Amanda is the nurse for the group, and a strong

and tough nurse she truly is.
Even when no one is sick she
will find something wrong
so she can cure it. The big
moments of her life are
giving shots. Each time she
pulls that long needle from
her little black bag, she gets
a crooked little smile on
her face and a devilish gleam
in her eye. Klaus told me
no man, woman or child is safe then. But it is a
different story when she has to travel by boat. She is
so afraid of the water that the minute she steps into
the boat, she lays down on the bottom, hiding under a
blanket, very quiet and shaking with fear. This is the
only time Amanda is quiet according to Klaus.''

''Why does Lena, the duck, always follow Olaf like
a shadow?'' Janet asked.

''Well, Olaf is the animal lover of the Ströms,'' I
began. ''He knows how to talk to animals and he helps

them whenever they are in trouble. They, in return, help him. Animals come whenever Olaf whistles for them. This whistle is something to see, Janet. He puts both feet squarely on the ground, fills his body full of air until he is almost bursting. Then he leans backward and blows a whistle through his teeth so hard that his whole body shakes. He face turns bright red and you think his mustache is going to jump right off. Everything, unless nailed down, is sent flying and you can hear this whistle for miles.''

"One day Olaf was helping some of the animals in the marsh by the edge of the forest when he came upon a nest. It had been deserted by the mother. Something must have attacked it and broken three of the eggs. Olaf carefully picked up the fourth egg, and holding the cold egg to his ear, he listened for sounds of life. Although he heard nothing, he thought there might be a chance to save the baby inside if he could keep the egg warm.

"Upon arriving home, Olaf built a little nest for the egg, and for the next two weeks he sat on it, just like a mother would do. To everyone's surprise, the egg hatched, and the baby duck was named Lena. Lena doesn't seem to know she's a duck. She thinks she is a Ström. Olaf, sometimes displeased with Lena's peskiness, said the next time he finds an egg, he is going to give it to Max, the skunk, to hatch.''

Janet quickly came to Lena's defense by saying, "I think she is a nice little duck."

"I think so too," I replied. "She helps Ingrid, Max and Fritz, the baby racoon, test the toys to make sure they're working properly."

"Oh, yes" Janet said, "how could I ever forget seeing a duck testing boats with so much energy."

Our eyes were now very heavy and soon we were asleep.

The following morning we were awakened by Nasha's loud barking. No amount of scolding or talking would quiet her. She continued to bark and run back and forth between the lake and the house. We dressed quickly to see what was making Nasha so excited.

Following Nasha to the lake, we were shocked to see three small boats smashed and washed up on shore. I could see the fear in Janet's face as she grabbed my hand. "Oh no! I am sure these boats belong to the Ströms. Something terrible must have happened."

Nasha was already running up the beach to our own boat and we ran after her.

"Hurry," I shouted to Janet. When Janet and I reached the boat, Nasha was already in it. She knew where we had to go. As soon as we rowed out on the lake, Nasha, at the front of the boat, her nose to the wind, tried to find a familiar smell. All the while she whimpered and whined.

"Janet, I am going to row towards their home," I said, "but keep looking on the water for any sign of them. Maybe something happened to them here."

The wind was blowing stronger on the lake. Bucking the wind, it seemed to take forever to reach the other side. Near the

mouth of the stream we heard loud
roaring, crashing, and smashing. We
could only think the worst. Slug Hog
had returned. As we come closer, we
could see Max, the skunk, and Oskar in
a tree by the shore. They were waving to
us. Rowing toward them, we heard Oskar
shout above the noise:

Come and draw near,
But no need to hurry.
Though Slug Hog is here,
There's no cause to worry.

Suddenly, there were two loud *CRACKS.* Then, the forest was completely quiet. Not a sound was to be heard and nothing was moving.

We turned towards Oskar when he began clapping his hands. Then, we saw everyone come running through the snow from all their hiding places. They were yelling and shouting and hugging each other. They started singing, "We did it. We did it. We did it."

They told us how the devilish Slug Hog had come tearing up the beach smashing their boats which then blew to the other shore where we had found them. Then the mean, old Slug Hog thundered toward their homes looking for the storehouse of food. This time they had a trap ready for him. All of the food was put inside a hollow tree with one round hole on the side. They knew that the horrible, selfish beast would find it. Johan and Klaus waited in the tree for him to poke his head through the hole for the food. When he did, they slammed the trap shut, locking his horns inside the tree. This time the awful, mean beast couldn't get loose without tearing his horns loose. If he didn't have his horns, he wouldn't have any power. So poor old Slug Hog had to decide if he would stay there stuck forever or tear his horns out and forever be like a *baby*, weak and powerless to hurt anyone or anything ever again.

54

Stig spoke up saying, "No matter what the Slug Hog decides, we don't have to worry about him anymore. Let's get the boats we have hidden and go finish the toys. Then, we shall have two reasons to celebrate tonight."

That night when all the toys were finished, we had a celebration that will never be forgotten. Before the Ströms left, Janet and I thanked each and every one for their help. We told them how much we appreciated their friendship. They, in turn, said the plans and the toys were now ours. They hoped the toys would bring as much joy to our grandchildren as they had to their children. It was sad to see them leave, not knowing if we would ever see them again.

We haven't. Although one very quiet summer evening just before dark we heard their beautiful music floating across the lake, and we knew that all was well with them.

THE END

yip

Authors' Note:

We know this story is hard to believe,
but it's the true story of how we
received the Ström toys. Oh, by the
way, did you wonder what happened
to old Slug Hog? Yes, he got his head
out, but without his horns, and he
now plays in the forest like a puppy.
Yes, an ugly one!

THE STRÖM TOYS
AND PLANS

SAIL MAKER

BAKERY

RESTAURANT

58

1. Marina
2. Town Buildings
3. Sailboats
4. Power Boats
5. Work Boats
6. Stern Wheeler
7. Side Wheeler
8. Car Ferry

MYSTIC SEAPORT (pages 58-59)
Here the owner is captain and harbor-master of all that moves. Makes shipping schedules. Sells tickets for river boat rides. Directs cargo. Loads and unloads barges. Boats can be duplicated to enlarge the fleet. This marina can grow and grow and grow and will provide years of continuous enjoyment.

CAR FERRY

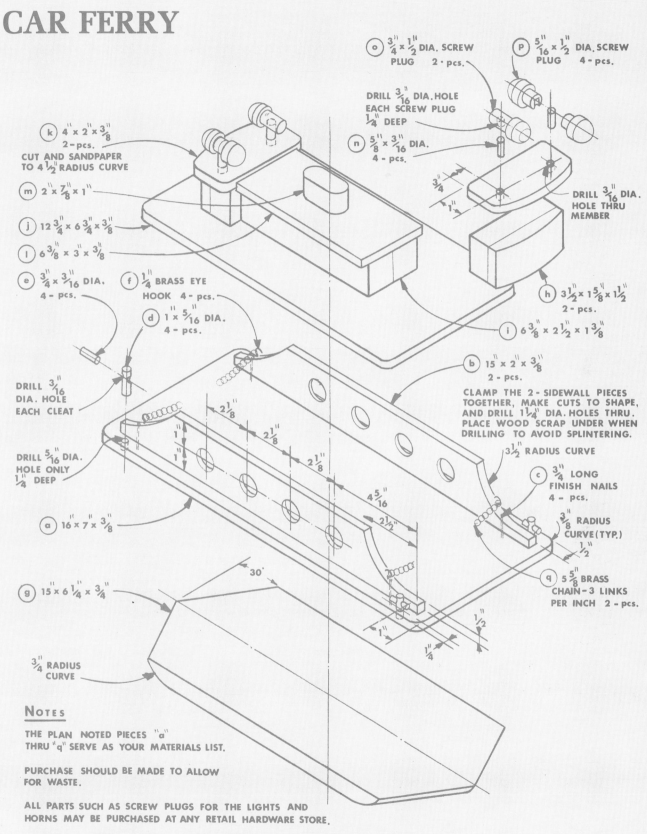

o $\frac{3}{4}" \times \frac{1}{2}"$ DIA. SCREW PLUG 2 · pcs.

p $\frac{5}{16}" \times \frac{1}{2}"$ DIA. SCREW PLUG 4 · pcs.

DRILL $\frac{3}{16}"$ DIA. HOLE EACH SCREW PLUG $\frac{1}{4}"$ DEEP

n $\frac{5}{8}" \times \frac{3}{16}"$ DIA. 4 · pcs.

k $4" \times 2" \times \frac{3}{8}"$ 2 · pcs.
CUT AND SANDPAPER TO $4\frac{1}{2}"$ RADIUS CURVE

m $2" \times 7\frac{7}{8}" \times 1"$

j $12\frac{3}{4}" \times 6\frac{3}{4}" \times \frac{3}{8}"$

l $6\frac{3}{8}" \times 3" \times \frac{3}{8}"$

e $\frac{3}{4}" \times \frac{3}{16}"$ DIA. 4 · pcs.

f $\frac{1}{4}"$ BRASS EYE HOOK 4 · pcs.

d $1" \times \frac{5}{16}"$ DIA. 4 · pcs.

DRILL $\frac{3}{16}"$ HOLE THRU MEMBER

h $3\frac{1}{2}" \times 1\frac{5}{8}" \times 1\frac{1}{2}"$ 2 · pcs.

i $6\frac{3}{8}" \times 2\frac{1}{2}" \times 1\frac{3}{8}"$

b $15" \times 2" \times \frac{3}{8}"$ 2 · pcs.

CLAMP THE 2 · SIDEWALL PIECES TOGETHER, MAKE CUTS TO SHAPE, AND DRILL $1\frac{1}{4}"$ DIA. HOLES THRU. PLACE WOOD SCRAP UNDER WHEN DRILLING TO AVOID SPLINTERING.

DRILL $\frac{3}{16}"$ DIA. HOLE EACH CLEAT

DRILL $\frac{5}{16}"$ DIA. HOLE ONLY $\frac{1}{4}"$ DEEP

$2\frac{1}{8}"$

$2\frac{1}{8}"$

$2\frac{1}{8}"$

$4\frac{5}{16}"$

$2\frac{1}{2}"$

$3\frac{1}{2}"$ RADIUS CURVE

c $\frac{3}{4}"$ LONG FINISH NAILS 4 · pcs.

$\frac{3}{8}"$ RADIUS CURVE (TYP.)

$\frac{1}{2}"$

a $16" \times 7" \times \frac{3}{8}"$

q $5\frac{5}{8}"$ BRASS CHAIN · 3 LINKS PER INCH 2 · pcs.

g $15" \times 6\frac{1}{4}" \times \frac{3}{4}"$

$30°$

$1"$

$1\frac{1}{4}"$

$1\frac{1}{2}"$

$\frac{3}{4}"$ RADIUS CURVE

Notes

THE PLAN NOTED PIECES "a" THRU "q" SERVE AS YOUR MATERIALS LIST.

PURCHASE SHOULD BE MADE TO ALLOW FOR WASTE.

ALL PARTS SUCH AS SCREW PLUGS FOR THE LIGHTS AND HORNS MAY BE PURCHASED AT ANY RETAIL HARDWARE STORE.

NOTE THAT PART "h" CONSISTS OF 1" AND $\frac{5}{8}"$ THICK MEMBERS LAMINATED TOGETHER. PART "i" CONSISTS OF TWO $1\frac{1}{4}"$ THICK MEMBERS LAMINATED.

USE POLYURETHANE SEALER OVERALL. PAINT AS PICTURED OR PER YOUR DESIRE. USE TWO COATS SPAR WATERPROOF VARNISH (THIRD COAT TO BOAT BOTTOM).

SAILBOAT

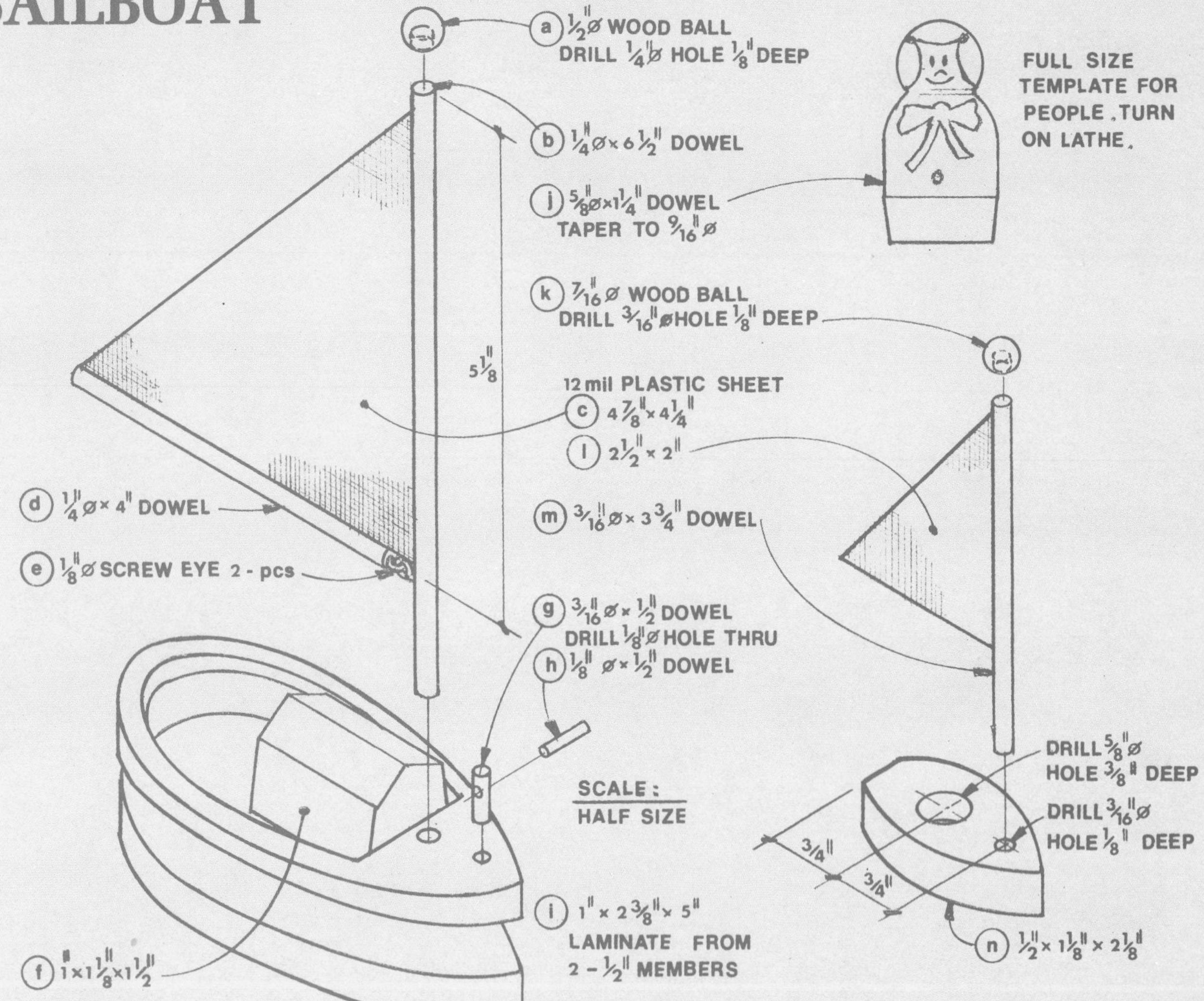

(a) 1/2"Ø WOOD BALL
DRILL 1/4"Ø HOLE 1/8" DEEP
(b) 1/4"Ø × 6 1/2" DOWEL
(j) 5/8"Ø × 1 1/4" DOWEL
TAPER TO 9/16"Ø
(k) 7/16Ø WOOD BALL
DRILL 3/16"Ø HOLE 1/8" DEEP
5 1/8
12 mil PLASTIC SHEET
(c) 4 7/8" × 4 1/4"
(l) 2 1/2" × 2"
(m) 3/16"Ø × 3 3/4" DOWEL
(d) 1/4"Ø × 4" DOWEL
(e) 1/8"Ø SCREW EYE 2 - pcs
(g) 3/16"Ø × 1/2" DOWEL
DRILL 1/8"Ø HOLE THRU
(h) 1/8" Ø × 1/2" DOWEL
SCALE: HALF SIZE
DRILL 5/8"Ø HOLE 3/8" DEEP
DRILL 3/16"Ø HOLE 1/8" DEEP
3/4"
3/4"
(i) 1" × 2 3/8" × 5"
LAMINATE FROM 2 - 1/2" MEMBERS
(f) 1" × 1 1/8" × 1 1/2"
(n) 1/2" × 1 1/8" × 2 1/8"
FULL SIZE TEMPLATE FOR PEOPLE. TURN ON LATHE.

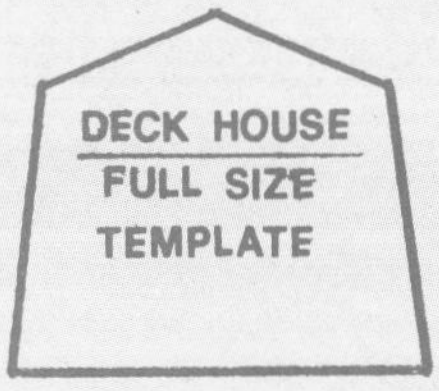

DECK HOUSE
FULL SIZE TEMPLATE

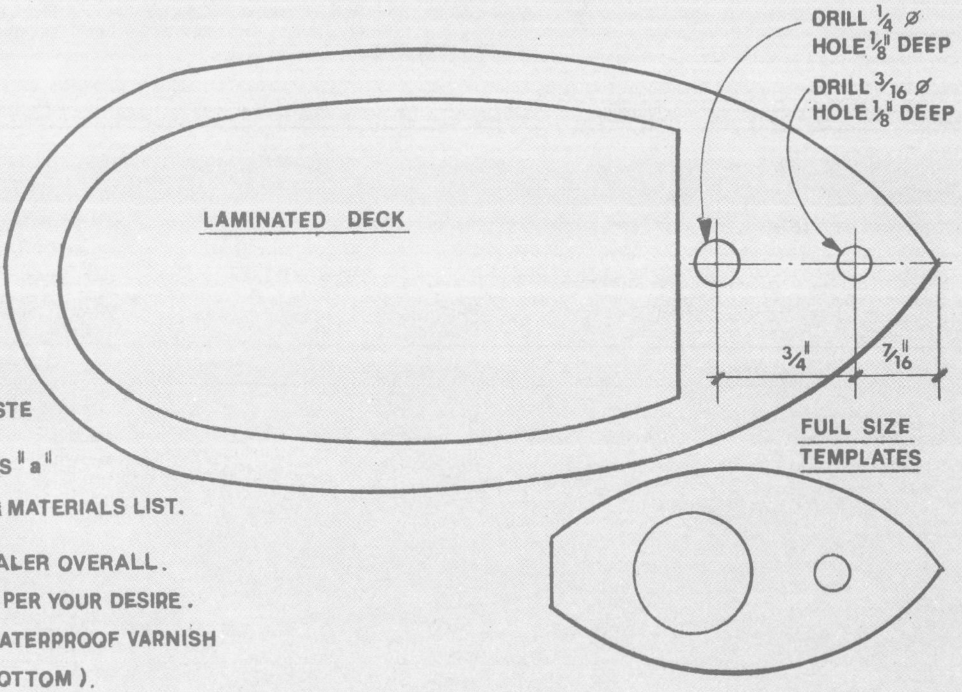

DRILL 1/4 Ø HOLE 1/8" DEEP
DRILL 3/16 Ø HOLE 1/8" DEEP
LAMINATED DECK
3/4"
7/16"
FULL SIZE TEMPLATES

NOTES:

PURCHASE SHOULD BE MADE TO ALLOW FOR WASTE

THE PLAN NOTED PIECES "a" THRU "n" SERVE AS YOUR MATERIALS LIST.

USE POLYURETHANE SEALER OVERALL.
PAINT AS PICTURED OR PER YOUR DESIRE.
USE TWO COATS SPAR WATERPROOF VARNISH (THIRD COAT TO BOAT BOTTOM).

MARINA HOME

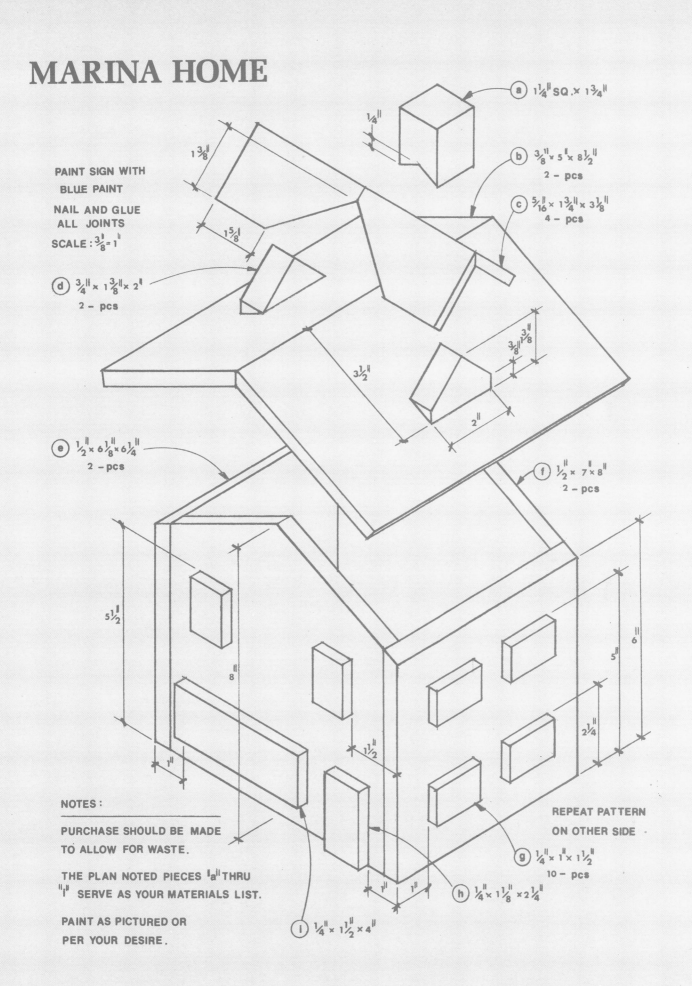

PAINT SIGN WITH
BLUE PAINT
NAIL AND GLUE
ALL JOINTS
SCALE: $\frac{3}{8}$" = 1"

ⓐ $1\frac{1}{4}$" SQ. × $1\frac{3}{4}$"

ⓑ $\frac{3}{8}$" × 5" × $8\frac{1}{2}$"
2 – pcs

ⓒ $\frac{5}{16}$" × $1\frac{3}{4}$" × $3\frac{1}{8}$"
4 – pcs

ⓓ $\frac{3}{4}$" × $1\frac{3}{8}$" × 2"
2 – pcs

ⓔ $\frac{1}{2}$" × $6\frac{1}{8}$" × $6\frac{1}{4}$"
2 – pcs

ⓕ $\frac{1}{2}$" × 7" × 8"
2 – pcs

ⓖ $\frac{1}{4}$" × 1" × $1\frac{1}{2}$"
10 – pcs

ⓗ $\frac{1}{4}$" × $1\frac{1}{8}$" × $2\frac{1}{4}$"

ⓘ $\frac{1}{4}$" × $1\frac{1}{2}$" × 4"

REPEAT PATTERN
ON OTHER SIDE

NOTES:

PURCHASE SHOULD BE MADE
TO ALLOW FOR WASTE.

THE PLAN NOTED PIECES "a" THRU
"I" SERVE AS YOUR MATERIALS LIST.

PAINT AS PICTURED OR
PER YOUR DESIRE.

63

BARGE

GRAIN SACK

(j) ½" × 2¼" COTTON
(k) 4" × 6" COTTON FLANNEL
FOLD AND SEW 2 SIDES OF
SACK, REVERSE, AND FILL
WITH CRUSHED STONE.
FOLD TOP BAND AND SEW
ONTO SACK TO CLOSE.

(a) $\frac{3}{16}$"Ø × 1" DOWEL
(VERTICAL)

(b) ¼" × 1¾" × 3
DRILL $\frac{3}{16}$"Ø HOLE THRU

(c) 1⅛" SQ. × 2½"

1⅛"

(d) 1½" × 2¼" × 4 LAMINATE
FROM 2-1⅛" MEMBERS

(e) ½" × 1½" × 10¼"
2 – pcs

¼"

(g)
½" × 4" × 7¼"

CARGO

(l) 1¼" × 3½" × 3⅞"
2 – pcs

(m) 1¼" × 3½" × 2"
4 – pcs

1⅞"

1"

1"

DRILL PILOT HOLE
FOR "n".
DRILL ⅝"Ø × ⅝" HOLE
IN BOTTOM

1"

(n) ⅜"Ø BRASS
SCREW EYE
8 – pcs

(h) $\frac{5}{16}$"Ø × ¾" DOWEL 4 – pcs
DRILL $\frac{3}{16}$"Ø HOLE THRU

(i) $\frac{3}{16}$"Ø × ¾" DOWEL
4 – pcs

DRILL $\frac{5}{16}$"Ø HOLE
⅛" DEEP

¼"

⅜"

(f) ¾" × 1½" × 4"

BEVEL
¾" @ 45°

NOTES

THE PLAN NOTED PIECES "a" THRU
"n" SERVE AS YOUR MATERIALS LIST.

PURCHASE SHOULD BE MADE
TO ALLOW FOR WASTE.

USE POLYURETHANE SEALER OVERALL.
PAINT AS PICTURED OR PER YOUR DESIRE.
USE TWO COATS SPAR WATERPROOF VARNISH
(THIRD COAT TO BOAT BOTTOM)

MARINA DOCK

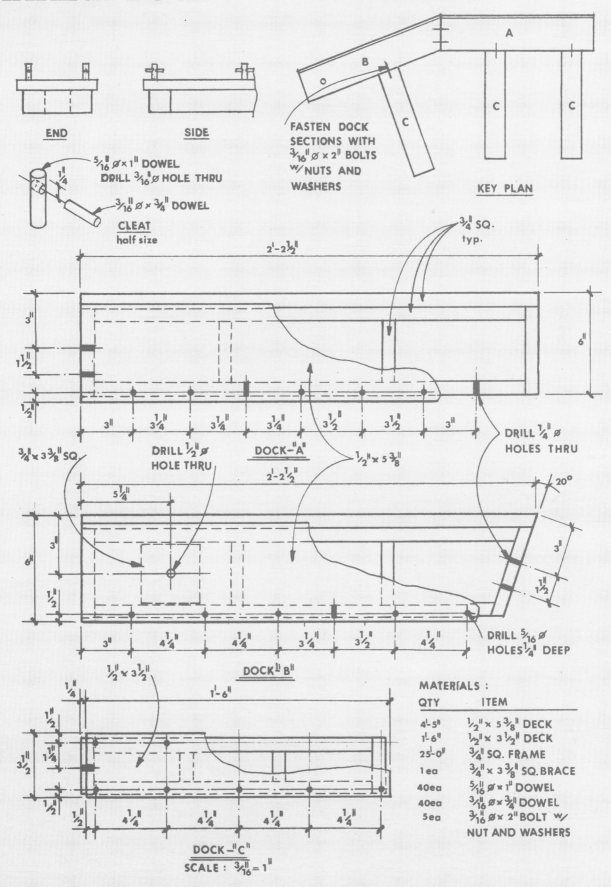

END

SIDE

5/16" ∅ × 1" DOWEL
DRILL 3/16" ∅ HOLE THRU

3/16" ∅ × 3/4" DOWEL

CLEAT
half size

FASTEN DOCK
SECTIONS WITH
3/16" ∅ × 2" BOLTS
w/ NUTS AND
WASHERS

KEY PLAN

3/4" SQ.
typ.

2'-2 1/2"

3"

1 1/2"

1/2"

6"

3" 1 3/4" 3 1/4" 3 1/4" 3 1/2" 3 1/2" 3"

DRILL 1/4" ∅
HOLES THRU

3/4" × 3 3/8" SQ

DRILL 1/2" ∅
HOLE THRU

DOCK-"A"

2'-2 1/2"

1/2" × 5 3/8"

20°

5 1/4"

6"

3"

3"

1 1/2"

1 1/2"

3" 4 1/4" 4 1/4" 3 1/4" 3 1/2" 4 1/4"

DRILL 5/16" ∅
HOLES 1/4" DEEP

DOCK "B"

1/2" × 3 1/2"

1-6"

1/4"

1 1/2"
1 1/4"

3 1/2"

1 1/4"

1/2"

1/2" 4 1/4" 4 1/4" 4 1/4" 4 1/4"

DOCK-"C"
SCALE : 3/16" = 1"

MATERIALS :

QTY	ITEM
4'-5"	1/2" × 5 3/8" DECK
1'-6"	1/2" × 3 1/2" DECK
25'-0"	3/4" SQ. FRAME
1 ea	3/4" × 3 3/8" SQ. BRACE
40 ea	5/16" ∅ × 1" DOWEL
40 ea	3/16" ∅ × 3/4" DOWEL
5 ea	3/16" ∅ × 2" BOLT w/ NUT AND WASHERS

MARINA CRANE

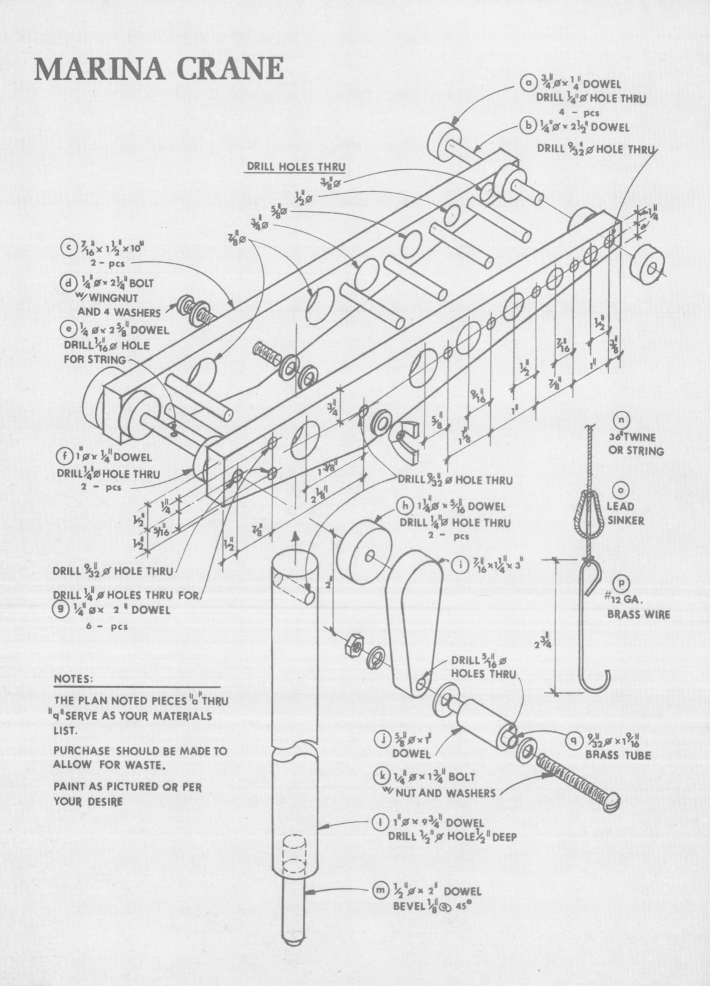

(a) $\frac{3}{4}"\emptyset \times \frac{1}{4}"$ DOWEL
DRILL $\frac{1}{2}"\emptyset$ HOLE THRU
4 – pcs

(b) $\frac{1}{4}"\emptyset \times 2\frac{1}{2}"$ DOWEL
DRILL $\frac{9}{32}"\emptyset$ HOLE THRU

DRILL HOLES THRU
$\frac{3}{8}"\emptyset$
$\frac{1}{2}"\emptyset$
$\frac{5}{8}"\emptyset$
$\frac{3}{4}"\emptyset$
$\frac{7}{8}"\emptyset$

(c) $\frac{7}{16}" \times 1\frac{1}{2}" \times 10"$
2 – pcs

(d) $\frac{1}{4}"\emptyset \times 2\frac{1}{4}"$ BOLT
w/ WINGNUT
AND 4 WASHERS

(e) $\frac{1}{4}\emptyset \times 2\frac{5}{8}"$ DOWEL
DRILL $\frac{1}{16}\emptyset$ HOLE
FOR STRING

(f) $1"\emptyset \times \frac{1}{4}"$ DOWEL
DRILL $\frac{1}{4}"\emptyset$ HOLE THRU
2 – pcs

DRILL $\frac{9}{32}"\emptyset$ HOLE THRU

DRILL $\frac{1}{4}"\emptyset$ HOLES THRU FOR

(g) $\frac{1}{4}"\emptyset \times 2"$ DOWEL
6 – pcs

DRILL $\frac{9}{32}"\emptyset$ HOLE THRU

(h) $1\frac{1}{4}"\emptyset \times \frac{5}{16}"$ DOWEL
DRILL $\frac{1}{4}"\emptyset$ HOLE THRU
2 – pcs

(i) $\frac{7}{16}" \times 1\frac{1}{4}" \times 3"$

(n) 36" TWINE OR STRING

(o) LEAD SINKER

(p) #12 GA. BRASS WIRE

DRILL $\frac{5}{16}"\emptyset$ HOLES THRU

(j) $\frac{5}{8}"\emptyset \times 1"$ DOWEL

(k) $\frac{1}{4}"\emptyset \times 1\frac{3}{4}"$ BOLT
w/ NUT AND WASHERS

(q) $\frac{9}{32}"\emptyset \times 1\frac{9}{16}"$ BRASS TUBE

(l) $1"\emptyset \times 9\frac{3}{4}"$ DOWEL
DRILL $\frac{1}{2}"\emptyset$ HOLE $\frac{1}{2}"$ DEEP

(m) $\frac{1}{2}"\emptyset \times 2"$ DOWEL
BEVEL $\frac{1}{8}"$ @ 45°

NOTES:

THE PLAN NOTED PIECES "a" THRU "q" SERVE AS YOUR MATERIALS LIST.

PURCHASE SHOULD BE MADE TO ALLOW FOR WASTE.

PAINT AS PICTURED OR PER YOUR DESIRE

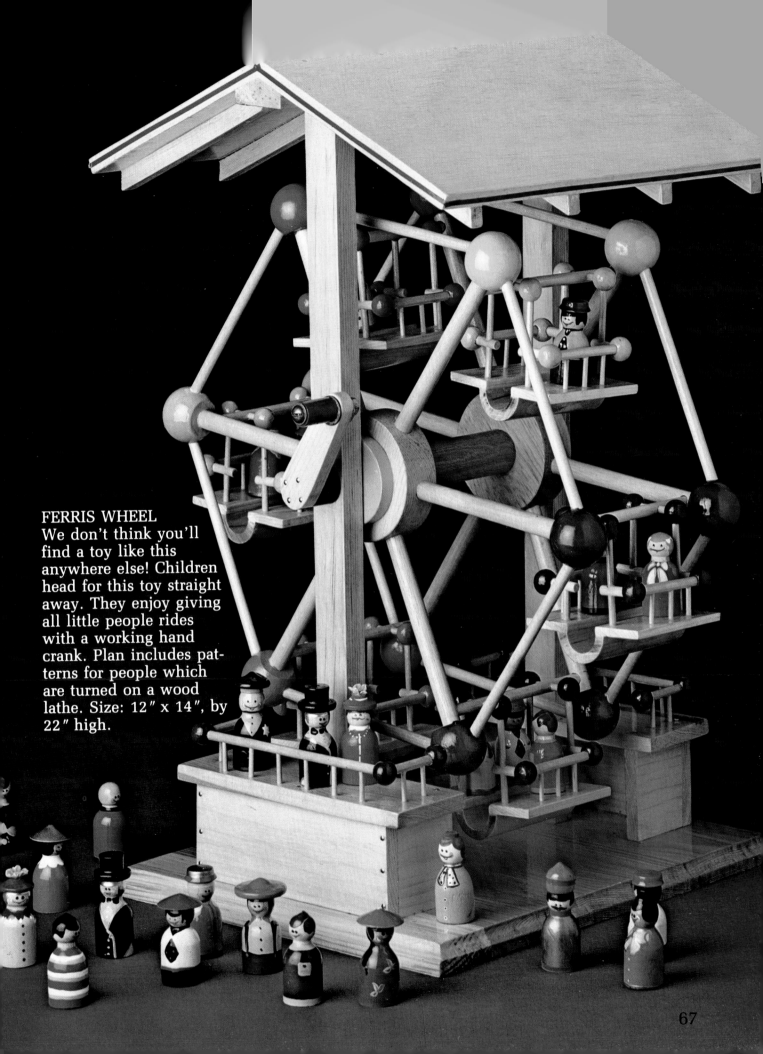

FERRIS WHEEL
We don't think you'll find a toy like this anywhere else! Children head for this toy straight away. They enjoy giving all little people rides with a working hand crank. Plan includes patterns for people which are turned on a wood lathe. Size: 12″ x 14″, by 22″ high.

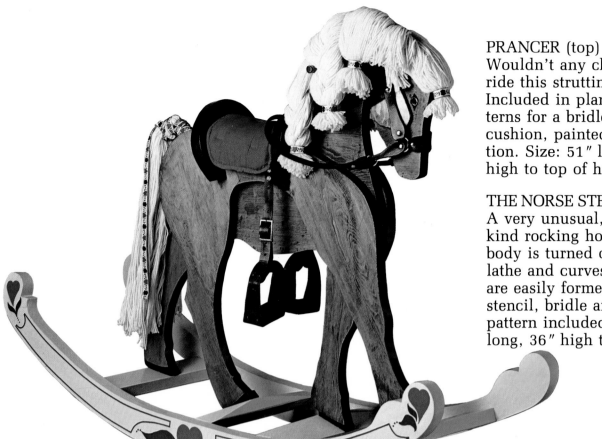

PRANCER (top)
Wouldn't any child love to ride this strutting horse? Included in plan are patterns for a bridle, stirrups, cushion, painted decoration. Size: 51″ long, 38″ high to top of head.

THE NORSE STEED (bottom)
A very unusual, one-of-a-kind rocking horse. The body is turned on a wood lathe and curves on base are easily formed. Painting stencil, bridle and cushion pattern included. Size: 40″ long, 36″ high to top of head.

TUMBLEWEED

A durable, all-wood rocking horse with a smooth, easy motion. Youngsters will like to crawl through it, and climb over it as much as they will like rocking on it. Mini-plan on pages 70-71. Size: 39″ long, 23″ high.

TUMBLEWEED

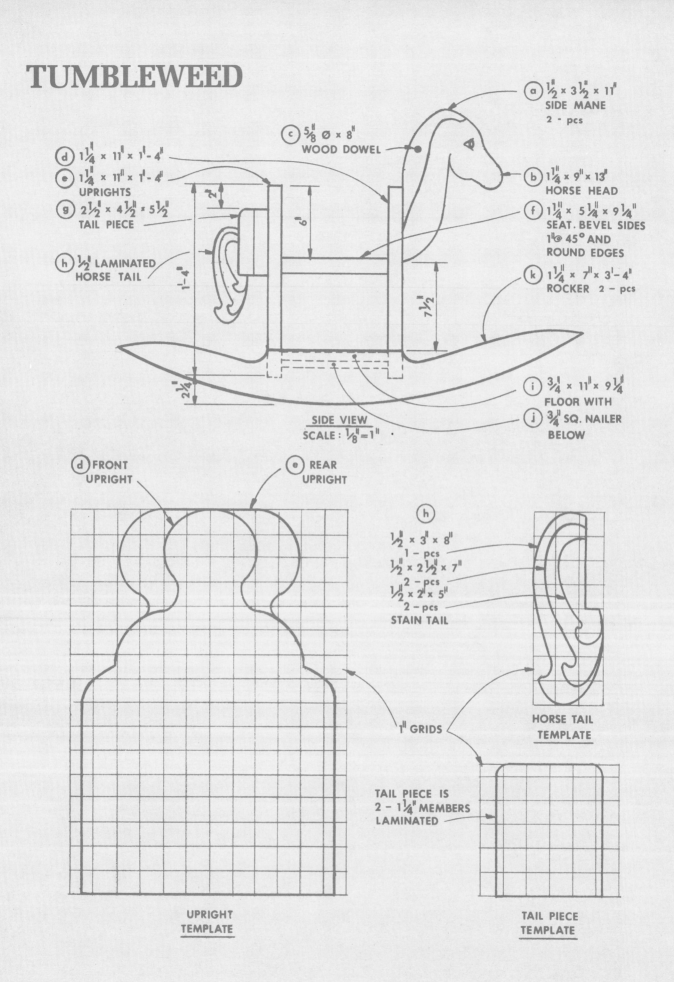

(a) $\frac{1}{2}" \times 3\frac{1}{2}" \times 11"$
SIDE MANE
2 - pcs

(c) $\frac{5}{8}" \varnothing \times 8"$
WOOD DOWEL

(d) $1\frac{1}{4}" \times 11" \times 1'-4"$
(e) $1\frac{1}{4}" \times 11" \times 1'-4"$
UPRIGHTS

(g) $2\frac{1}{4}" \times 4\frac{1}{2}" \times 5\frac{1}{2}"$
TAIL PIECE

(h) $\frac{1}{2}"$ LAMINATED
HORSE TAIL

(b) $1\frac{1}{4}" \times 9" \times 13"$
HORSE HEAD

(f) $1\frac{1}{4}" \times 5\frac{1}{4}" \times 9\frac{1}{4}"$
SEAT. BEVEL SIDES
1" @ 45° AND
ROUND EDGES

(k) $1\frac{1}{4}" \times 7" \times 3'-4"$
ROCKER 2 – pcs

(i) $\frac{3}{4}" \times 11" \times 9\frac{1}{4}"$
FLOOR WITH

(j) $\frac{3}{4}"$ SQ. NAILER
BELOW

SIDE VIEW
SCALE: $\frac{1}{8}" = 1"$

(d) FRONT
UPRIGHT

(e) REAR
UPRIGHT

(h)
$\frac{1}{2}" \times 3" \times 8"$
1 - pcs
$\frac{1}{2}" \times 2\frac{1}{2}" \times 7"$
2 - pcs
$\frac{1}{2}" \times 2" \times 5"$
2 - pcs
STAIN TAIL

1" GRIDS

HORSE TAIL
TEMPLATE

UPRIGHT
TEMPLATE

TAIL PIECE IS
2 – $1\frac{1}{4}"$ MEMBERS
LAMINATED

TAIL PIECE
TEMPLATE

PROCEDURE FOR HORSE HEAD

CUT OUT HEAD FROM $1\frac{1}{4}''$ STOCK AND MANE FROM $\frac{1}{2}''$ STOCK AND GLUE (CLAMPED). NOTCH HEAD AND DRILL HOLE FOR DOWEL. GLUE DOWEL IN PLACE. STAIN MANE AND DOWEL.

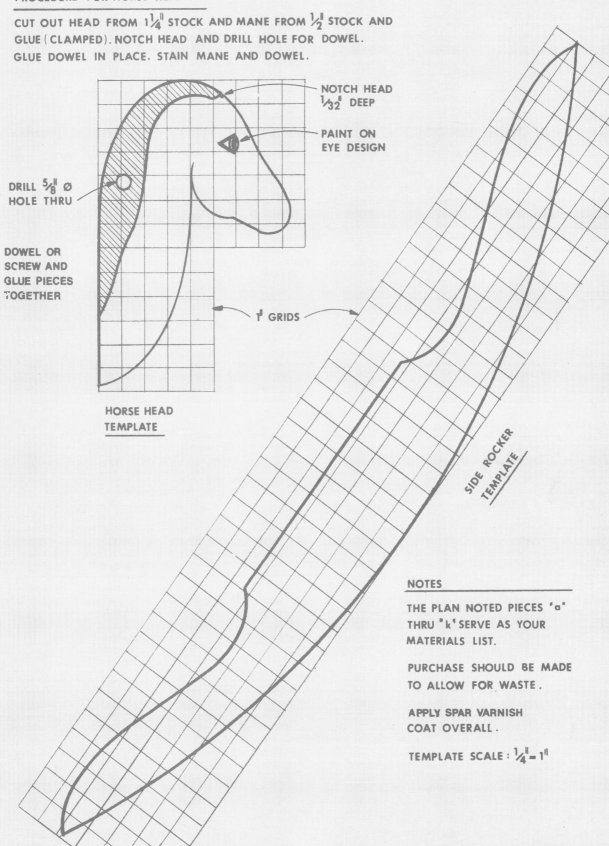

NOTCH HEAD $\frac{1}{32}''$ DEEP

PAINT ON EYE DESIGN

DRILL $\frac{5}{8}''$ Ø HOLE THRU

DOWEL OR SCREW AND GLUE PIECES TOGETHER

1" GRIDS

HORSE HEAD TEMPLATE

SIDE ROCKER TEMPLATE

NOTES

THE PLAN NOTED PIECES 'a' THRU 'k' SERVE AS YOUR MATERIALS LIST.

PURCHASE SHOULD BE MADE TO ALLOW FOR WASTE.

APPLY SPAR VARNISH COAT OVERALL.

TEMPLATE SCALE : $\frac{1}{4}''=1''$

BANK
Simple but intriguing. See if the kids can solve the mystery of the disappearing coins! Mini-plan below. Size: 5″ high, 4″ wide.

BANK

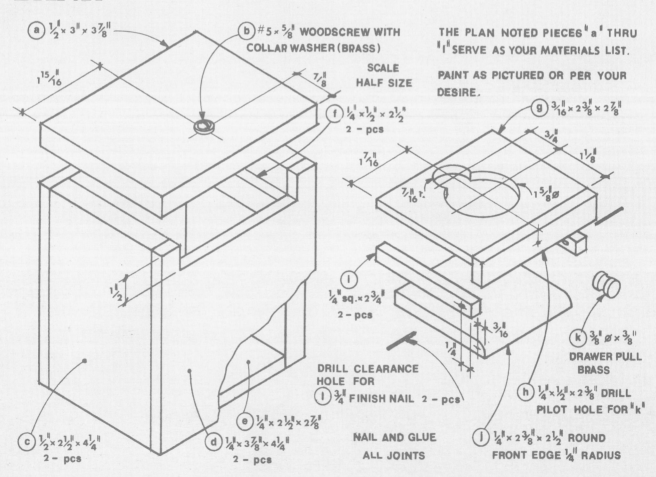

(a) $\frac{1}{2}$″ × 3″ × 3$\frac{7}{8}$″

(b) #5 × $\frac{5}{8}$″ WOODSCREW WITH COLLAR WASHER (BRASS)

SCALE HALF SIZE

THE PLAN NOTED PIECES "a" THRU "I" SERVE AS YOUR MATERIALS LIST.

PAINT AS PICTURED OR PER YOUR DESIRE.

$1\frac{15}{16}$″

$\frac{7}{8}$″

(f) $\frac{1}{4}$″ × $\frac{1}{2}$″ × $2\frac{1}{2}$″ 2 - pcs

(g) $\frac{3}{16}$″ × $2\frac{3}{8}$″ × $2\frac{7}{8}$″

$\frac{3}{4}$″

$1\frac{1}{8}$″

$\frac{7}{16}$″

$\frac{7}{16}$″ r.

$1\frac{5}{8}$″ ∅

$1\frac{1}{2}$″

(i) $\frac{1}{4}$″ sq. × $2\frac{3}{4}$″ 2 - pcs

$\frac{3}{16}$″

$\frac{1}{4}$″

(k) $\frac{3}{8}$″ ∅ × $\frac{3}{8}$″ DRAWER PULL BRASS

DRILL CLEARANCE HOLE FOR

(j) $\frac{3}{4}$″ FINISH NAIL 2 - pcs

(h) $\frac{1}{4}$″ × $\frac{1}{2}$″ × $2\frac{3}{8}$″ DRILL PILOT HOLE FOR "k"

(e) $\frac{1}{4}$″ × $2\frac{1}{2}$″ × $2\frac{7}{8}$″

NAIL AND GLUE

ALL JOINTS

(j) $\frac{1}{4}$″ × $2\frac{3}{8}$″ × $2\frac{1}{2}$″ ROUND FRONT EDGE $\frac{1}{4}$″ RADIUS

(c) $\frac{1}{2}$″ × $2\frac{1}{2}$″ × $4\frac{1}{4}$″ 2 - pcs

(d) $\frac{1}{4}$″ × $3\frac{7}{8}$″ × $4\frac{1}{4}$″ 2 - pcs

BENTWOOD DOLL BUGGY

This delightful all-lined doll buggy with its two-position wood shade hood is just the thing for your special little friend. A perfect buggy to show off a doll on a morning stroll. After the stroll, the doll can snuggle down in warmth, comfort and beauty for her afternoon nap. Wheels are turned on lathe. Bent wood is a simple system. Patterns for lining also included. Size: 12″ wide, 30″ high, and 30″ long, including handle.

THE STRÖM WAGON

A classic style, full-sized, all-wood wagon with laminated, curved handle. What a special gift for someone! Handles exceptionally well. Wood wheels are turned on a basic wood lathe. Size: 38″ long, 18″ wide.

CEMENT MIXER AND FRONT LOADER

Wow! Who else but a little Strom could have designed something like this? A big moving, rolling, mixing, cranking cement truck. A simple clutch allows a hand crank to load the mixer, then mix and unload. The unload chute has mix and unload positions. The trailer can be unhooked and a spring-loaded pedestal allows it to stand by itself when parked after a hard days work. It's easier to build than it looks. Size: 27" long, 17" high, 10" wide.

The Front End Loader is lots of fun and an easy-to-work mechanism, for digging and dumping. Mini-plan on pages 76 and 77. Size: 21" long, 7" wide, 9" high.

FRONT END LOADER

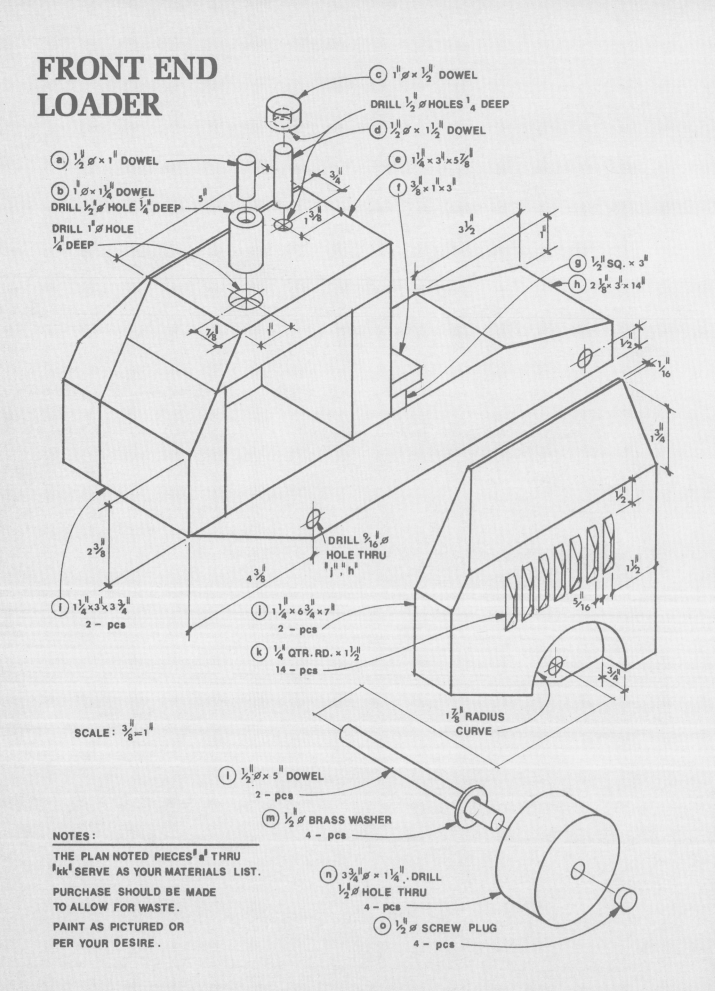

(c) 1″ø × 1/2″ DOWEL

DRILL 1/2″ø HOLES 1/4 DEEP

(d) 1/2″ø × 1 1/2″ DOWEL

(e) 1 1/4″ × 3″ × 5 7/8″

(f) 3/8″ × 1″ × 3″

(a) 1/2″ø × 1″ DOWEL

(b) 1″ø × 1 1/4″ DOWEL
DRILL 1/2″ø HOLE 1/4 DEEP

DRILL 1″ø HOLE 1/4 DEEP

5″

3/4″

1 3/8″

3 1/2″

1″

(g) 1/2″ SQ. × 3″

(h) 2 1/8″ × 3″ × 14″

1/2″

1/16″

1 3/4″

1/2″

1 1/2″

7/8″

1″

2 3/8″

5/16″

3/4″

DRILL 9/16″ø HOLE THRU "j", "h"

4 3/8″

(i) 1 1/4″ × 3″ × 3 3/4″
2 – pcs

(j) 1 1/4″ × 6 3/4″ × 7″
2 – pcs

(k) 1/4″ QTR. RD. × 1 1/2″
14 – pcs

1 7/8″ RADIUS CURVE

SCALE: 3/8″ = 1″

(l) 1/2″ø × 5″ DOWEL
2 – pcs

(m) 1/2″ø BRASS WASHER
4 – pcs

NOTES:

THE PLAN NOTED PIECES "a" THRU "kk" SERVE AS YOUR MATERIALS LIST.

PURCHASE SHOULD BE MADE TO ALLOW FOR WASTE.

PAINT AS PICTURED OR PER YOUR DESIRE.

(n) 3 3/4″ø × 1 1/4″. DRILL 1/2″ø HOLE THRU
4 – pcs

(o) 1/2″ø SCREW PLUG
4 – pcs

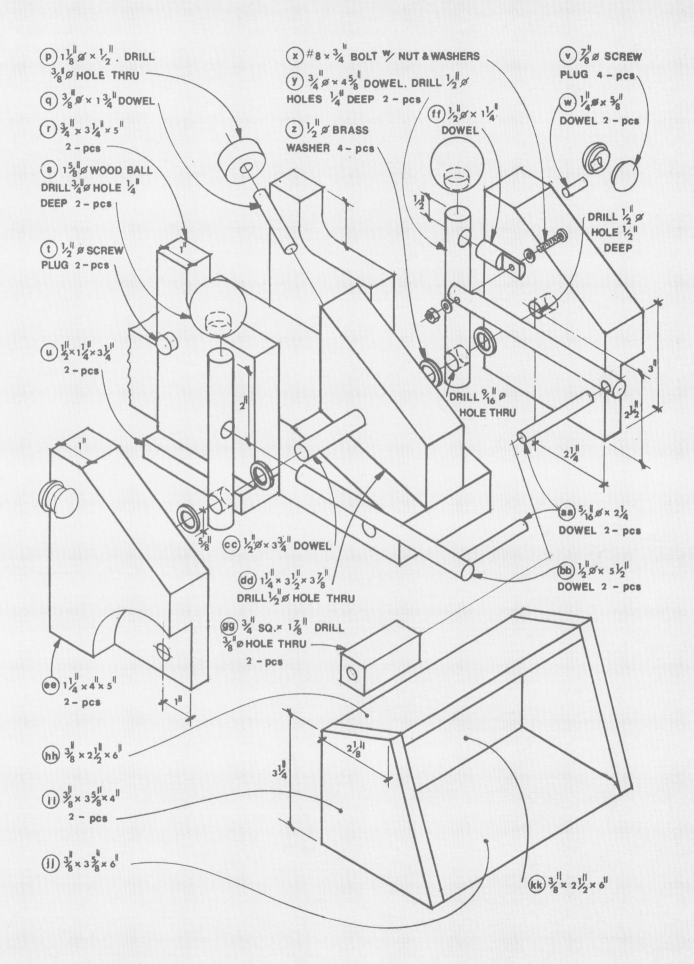

(p) $1\frac{1}{8}'' \varnothing \times \frac{1}{2}''$. DRILL $\frac{3}{8}'' \varnothing$ HOLE THRU

(q) $\frac{3}{8}'' \varnothing \times 1\frac{3}{4}''$ DOWEL

(r) $\frac{3}{4} \times 3\frac{1}{4} \times 5''$ 2 – pcs

(s) $1\frac{5}{8}'' \varnothing$ WOOD BALL DRILL $\frac{3}{4}'' \varnothing$ HOLE $\frac{1}{4}''$ DEEP 2 – pcs

(t) $\frac{1}{2}'' \varnothing$ SCREW PLUG 2 – pcs

(u) $1\frac{1}{2}'' \times 1\frac{1}{4}'' \times 3\frac{1}{4}''$ 2 – pcs

(x) $\#8 \times \frac{3}{4}''$ BOLT W/ NUT & WASHERS

(y) $\frac{3}{4}'' \varnothing \times 4\frac{5}{8}''$ DOWEL. DRILL $\frac{1}{2}'' \varnothing$ HOLES $\frac{1}{4}''$ DEEP 2 – pcs

(z) $\frac{1}{2}'' \varnothing$ BRASS WASHER 4 – pcs

(ff) $\frac{1}{2}'' \varnothing \times 1\frac{1}{4}''$ DOWEL

(v) $\frac{7}{8}'' \varnothing$ SCREW PLUG 4 – pcs

(w) $\frac{1}{4}'' \varnothing \times \frac{5}{8}''$ DOWEL 2 – pcs

DRILL $\frac{1}{2}'' \varnothing$ HOLE $\frac{1}{2}''$ DEEP

$\frac{1}{2}$

$1''$

$2''$

$3''$

$2\frac{1}{2}''$

$2\frac{1}{4}$

DRILL $\frac{9}{16}'' \varnothing$ HOLE THRU

(aa) $\frac{5}{16}'' \varnothing \times 2\frac{1}{4}$ DOWEL 2 – pcs

(bb) $\frac{1}{2}'' \varnothing \times 5\frac{1}{2}''$ DOWEL 2 – pcs

$1''$

$\frac{5}{8}''$

(cc) $\frac{1}{2}'' \varnothing \times 3\frac{3}{4}''$ DOWEL

(dd) $1\frac{1}{4}'' \times 3\frac{1}{2}'' \times 3\frac{7}{8}''$ DRILL $\frac{1}{2}'' \varnothing$ HOLE THRU

(gg) $\frac{3}{4}''$ SQ. $\times 1\frac{7}{8}''$ DRILL $\frac{3}{8}'' \varnothing$ HOLE THRU 2 – pcs

(ee) $1\frac{1}{4}'' \times 4'' \times 5''$ 2 – pcs

$1''$

(hh) $\frac{3}{8}'' \times 2\frac{1}{2}'' \times 6''$

(ii) $\frac{3}{8}'' \times 3\frac{5}{8}'' \times 4''$ 2 – pcs

(jj) $\frac{3}{8}'' \times 3\frac{3}{4}'' \times 6''$

$2\frac{1}{8}''$

$3\frac{1}{4}''$

(kk) $\frac{3}{8}'' \times 2\frac{1}{2}'' \times 6''$

This is a favorite. A tough truck and trailer for all those big jobs around the house, completes your truck fleet. Barrell plan included. Size: Trailer 8″ long, 7″ wide. Truck 19″ long, 7″ wide.

Fully workable boom retracts from 34″ to 19″, and is adjustable from a horizontal position up to about 60°. Color-coded hand cranks and brake knobs for easy co-ordination. Size: 14″ long, 9″ wide.

SAND CONVEYOR
A real classic in wooden toys! Oak buckets on an adjustable conveyor arm digs deep to load dump truck quickly. Has brake for holding conveyor arm at desired angle. Size: 28″ long, 14″ high.

TOW TRUCK
Heavy duty twin-stack truck with a
spring-loaded winch lock that will
hold a towed vehicle in any position.
Size: 17″ long, 7″ wide.

STEAM ROLLER
Old-fashioned steam roller and water wagon. Brass drive chain on wheel drives fly-wheel and wood piston back and forth. Steering wheel turns front roller. Size: 15″ long, 10″ high. Water wagon 10″ long.

BULLDOZER
Has an easy-working, up-and-down blade action which is controlled by the handle with the yellow ball. Simulated job sticks for steering, and instrument panel. Size: 13″ long, 8″ high.

STEAMROLLER

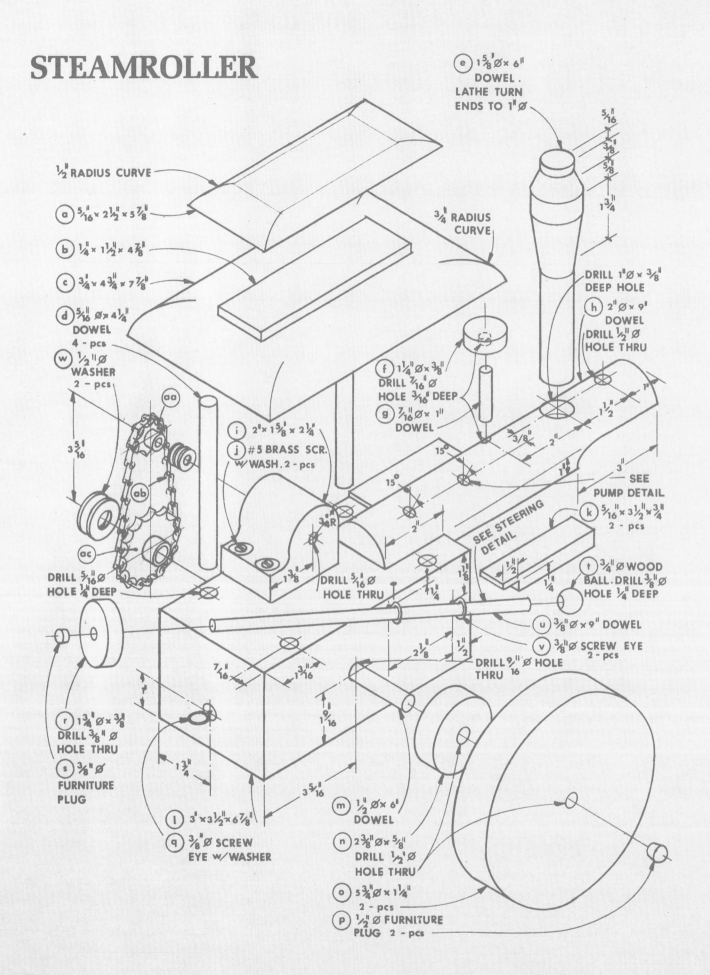

½" RADIUS CURVE

ⓐ $\frac{5}{16}$" × $2\frac{1}{2}$" × $5\frac{7}{8}$"

ⓑ $\frac{1}{4}$" × $1\frac{1}{4}$" × $4\frac{7}{8}$"

ⓒ $\frac{3}{4}$" × $4\frac{3}{4}$" × $7\frac{7}{8}$"

ⓓ $\frac{5}{16}$" Ø × $4\frac{1}{4}$" DOWEL 4 - pcs

ⓦ ½" Ø WASHER 2 - pcs

ⓔ $1\frac{5}{8}$" Ø × 6" DOWEL. LATHE TURN ENDS TO 1" Ø

$\frac{5}{16}$" $\frac{3}{8}$" $\frac{5}{8}$" $1\frac{3}{4}$"

DRILL 1" Ø × $\frac{3}{8}$" DEEP HOLE

ⓗ 2" Ø × 9" DOWEL DRILL ½" Ø HOLE THRU

¾" RADIUS CURVE

ⓕ $1\frac{1}{4}$" Ø × $\frac{3}{8}$" DRILL $\frac{7}{16}$" Ø HOLE $\frac{3}{16}$" DEEP

ⓖ $\frac{7}{16}$" Ø × 1" DOWEL

$3\frac{5}{16}$"

ⓐⓐ

ⓐⓑ

ⓐⓒ

ⓘ 2" × $1\frac{5}{8}$" × $2\frac{1}{4}$"

ⓙ #5 BRASS SCR. w/ WASH. 2 - pcs

DRILL $\frac{5}{16}$" Ø HOLE $\frac{1}{4}$" DEEP

$\frac{3}{4}$R

15°

15°

2"

2"

$\frac{3}{8}$"

$1\frac{1}{8}$"

$1\frac{1}{2}$"

1"

3"

SEE PUMP DETAIL

SEE STEERING DETAIL

ⓚ $\frac{5}{16}$" × $3\frac{1}{2}$" × $\frac{3}{4}$" 2 - pcs

$1\frac{1}{2}$"

$\frac{1}{4}$"

ⓣ $\frac{3}{4}$" Ø WOOD BALL. DRILL $\frac{3}{8}$" Ø HOLE $\frac{1}{4}$" DEEP

ⓢ

DRILL $\frac{5}{16}$" Ø HOLE THRU

$1\frac{3}{8}$"

$1\frac{1}{8}$"

$7\frac{1}{4}$"

ⓤ $\frac{3}{8}$" Ø × 9" DOWEL

ⓥ $\frac{3}{8}$" Ø SCREW EYE 2 - pcs

$7\frac{1}{16}$"

$1\frac{3}{16}$"

$2\frac{1}{8}$"

$1\frac{1}{2}$"

DRILL $\frac{9}{16}$" Ø HOLE THRU

ⓡ $1\frac{3}{4}$" Ø × $\frac{3}{8}$" DRILL $\frac{3}{8}$" Ø HOLE THRU

ⓢ $\frac{3}{8}$" Ø FURNITURE PLUG

$1\frac{3}{4}$"

$\frac{9}{16}$"

$3\frac{5}{16}$"

ⓛ 3" × $3\frac{1}{2}$" × $6\frac{7}{8}$"

ⓠ $\frac{3}{8}$" Ø SCREW EYE w/WASHER

ⓜ ½" Ø × 6" DOWEL

ⓝ $2\frac{3}{8}$" Ø × $\frac{5}{8}$" DRILL ½" Ø HOLE THRU

ⓞ $5\frac{3}{4}$" Ø × $1\frac{1}{4}$" 2 - pcs

ⓟ ½" Ø FURNITURE PLUG 2 - pcs

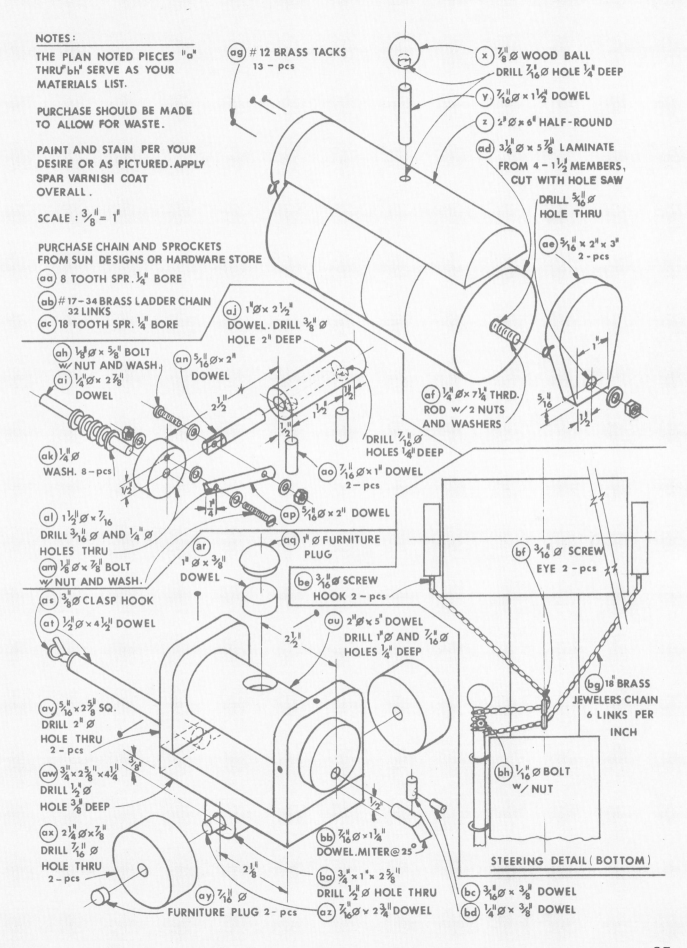

NOTES:

THE PLAN NOTED PIECES "a"
THRU "bh" SERVE AS YOUR
MATERIALS LIST.

PURCHASE SHOULD BE MADE
TO ALLOW FOR WASTE.

PAINT AND STAIN PER YOUR
DESIRE OR AS PICTURED. APPLY
SPAR VARNISH COAT
OVERALL.

SCALE : $\frac{3}{8}$" = 1"

PURCHASE CHAIN AND SPROCKETS
FROM SUN DESIGNS OR HARDWARE STORE

(aa) 8 TOOTH SPR. $\frac{1}{4}$" BORE

(ab) # 17-34 BRASS LADDER CHAIN
32 LINKS

(ac) 18 TOOTH SPR. $\frac{1}{4}$" BORE

(ah) $\frac{1}{8}$"Ø × $\frac{5}{8}$" BOLT
W/ NUT AND WASH.

(ai) $\frac{1}{4}$"Ø × 2$\frac{7}{8}$"
DOWEL

(ak) $\frac{1}{4}$"Ø
WASH. 8 – pcs

(al) 1$\frac{1}{2}$"Ø × $\frac{7}{16}$
DRILL $\frac{3}{16}$"Ø AND $\frac{1}{4}$"Ø
HOLES THRU

(am) $\frac{1}{8}$"Ø × $\frac{7}{8}$" BOLT
W/ NUT AND WASH.

(as) $\frac{3}{8}$" CLASP HOOK

(at) $\frac{1}{2}$"Ø × 4$\frac{1}{2}$" DOWEL

(av) $\frac{5}{16}$" × 2$\frac{5}{8}$" SQ.
DRILL 2"Ø
HOLE THRU
2 – pcs

(aw) $\frac{3}{4}$" × 2$\frac{5}{8}$" × 4$\frac{1}{4}$"
DRILL $\frac{1}{2}$"Ø
HOLE $\frac{3}{8}$" DEEP

(ax) 2$\frac{1}{4}$"Ø × $\frac{7}{8}$"
DRILL $\frac{7}{16}$"Ø
HOLE THRU
2 – pcs

(ay) $\frac{7}{16}$"Ø
FURNITURE PLUG 2 – pcs

(ag) # 12 BRASS TACKS
13 – pcs

(aj) 1"Ø × 2$\frac{1}{2}$"
DOWEL. DRILL $\frac{3}{8}$"Ø
HOLE 2" DEEP

(an) $\frac{5}{16}$"Ø × 2"
DOWEL

(ao) $\frac{7}{16}$"Ø × 1" DOWEL
2 – pcs

(ap) $\frac{5}{16}$"Ø × 2" DOWEL

(aq) 1"Ø FURNITURE
PLUG

(ar) 1"Ø × $\frac{3}{8}$"
DOWEL

(au) 2"Ø × 5" DOWEL
DRILL 1"Ø AND $\frac{7}{16}$"Ø
HOLES $\frac{1}{4}$" DEEP

(bb) $\frac{7}{16}$"Ø × 1$\frac{1}{4}$"
DOWEL. MITER @ 25°

(ba) $\frac{3}{4}$" × 1" × 2$\frac{5}{8}$"
DRILL $\frac{1}{2}$"Ø HOLE THRU

(az) $\frac{7}{16}$"Ø × 2$\frac{3}{4}$" DOWEL

(x) $\frac{7}{8}$"Ø WOOD BALL
DRILL $\frac{7}{16}$"Ø HOLE $\frac{1}{4}$" DEEP

(y) $\frac{7}{16}$"Ø × 1$\frac{1}{2}$" DOWEL

(z) 2"Ø × 6" HALF-ROUND

(ad) 3$\frac{1}{4}$"Ø × 5$\frac{5}{8}$" LAMINATE
FROM 4 – 1$\frac{1}{2}$" MEMBERS,
CUT WITH HOLE SAW
DRILL $\frac{5}{16}$"Ø
HOLE THRU

(ae) $\frac{5}{16}$" × 2" × 3"
2 – pcs

(af) $\frac{1}{4}$"Ø × 7$\frac{1}{4}$" THRD.
ROD W/ 2 NUTS
AND WASHERS

DRILL $\frac{7}{16}$"Ø
HOLES $\frac{1}{4}$" DEEP

(bf) $\frac{3}{16}$"Ø SCREW
EYE 2 – pcs

(be) $\frac{3}{16}$"Ø SCREW
HOOK 2 – pcs

(bg) 18" BRASS
JEWELERS CHAIN
6 LINKS PER
INCH

(bh) $\frac{1}{16}$"Ø BOLT
W/ NUT

STEERING DETAIL (BOTTOM)

(bc) $\frac{3}{16}$"Ø × $\frac{3}{8}$" DOWEL

(bd) $\frac{1}{4}$"Ø × $\frac{3}{8}$" DOWEL

85

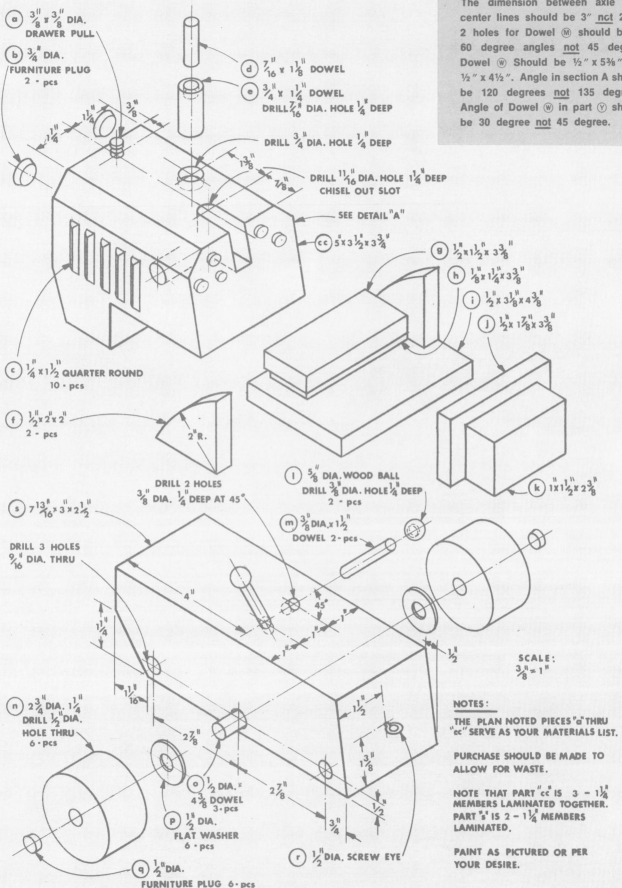

BULLDOZER

ⓐ ⅜" x ⅜" DIA. DRAWER PULL

ⓑ ¾" DIA. FURNITURE PLUG 2 - pcs

ⓓ 7/16" x 1⅛" DOWEL

ⓔ ¾" x 1¼" DOWEL DRILL 7/16" DIA. HOLE ¼" DEEP

DRILL ¾" DIA. HOLE ¼" DEEP

DRILL 11/16" DIA. HOLE 1¼" DEEP CHISEL OUT SLOT

SEE DETAIL "A"

ⓒⓒ 5" x 3½" x 3¾"

ⓖ ½" x 1½" x 3⅜"

ⓗ ⅛" x 1¼" x 3⅜"

ⓘ ½" x 3⅛" x 4⅜"

ⓙ ½" x 1⅞" x 3⅜"

ⓚ 1" x 1½" x 2⅜"

ⓒ ¼" x 1½" QUARTER ROUND 10 - pcs

ⓕ ½" x 2" x 2" 2 - pcs

2" R.

DRILL 2 HOLES ⅜" DIA. ¼" DEEP AT 45°

ⓛ ⅝" DIA. WOOD BALL DRILL ⅜" DIA. HOLE ¼" DEEP 2 - pcs

ⓜ ⅜" DIA. x 1½" DOWEL 2 - pcs

ⓢ 7 13/16" x 3" x 2½"

DRILL 3 HOLES 9/16" DIA. THRU

4"

1¼"

45°

1"

1"

1"

ⓝ 2¾" DIA. 1¼" DRILL ½" DIA. HOLE THRU 6 - pcs

1 1/16"

2⅞"

½"

ⓞ ½" DIA. x 4⅜" DOWEL 3 - pcs

ⓟ ½" DIA. FLAT WASHER 6 - pcs

2⅞"

1½"

1⅜"

½"

¾"

ⓡ ½" DIA. SCREW EYE

ⓠ ½" DIA. FURNITURE PLUG 6 - pcs

SCALE: ⅜" = 1"

NOTES:

THE PLAN NOTED PIECES "a" THRU "cc" SERVE AS YOUR MATERIALS LIST.

PURCHASE SHOULD BE MADE TO ALLOW FOR WASTE.

NOTE THAT PART "cc" IS 3 - 1¼" MEMBERS LAMINATED TOGETHER. PART "s" IS 2 - 1¼" MEMBERS LAMINATED.

PAINT AS PICTURED OR PER YOUR DESIRE.

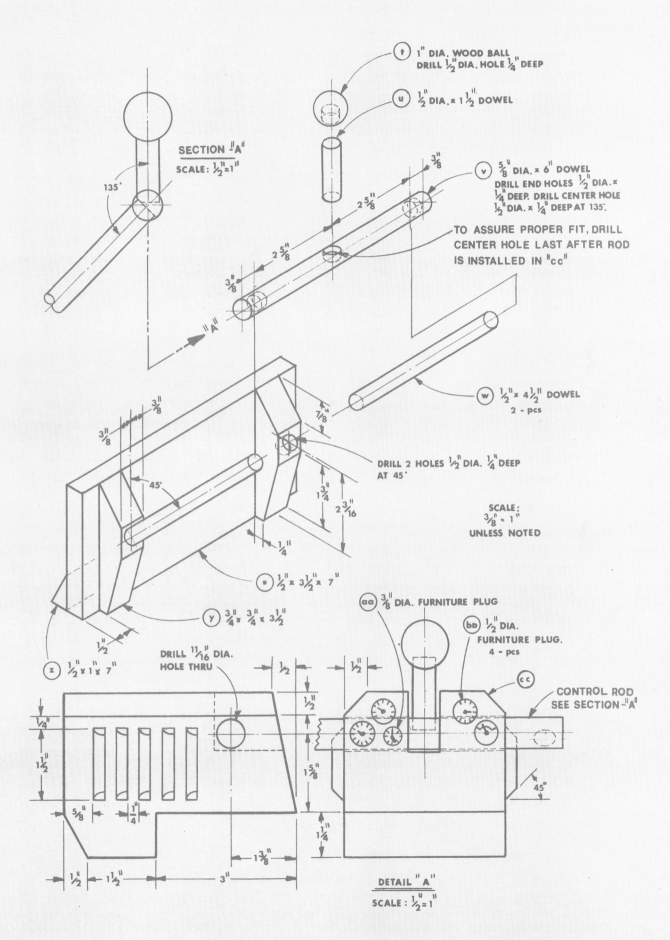

SECTION "A"
SCALE: 1/2"=1"

135°

t 1" DIA. WOOD BALL
   DRILL 1/2" DIA. HOLE 1/4" DEEP

u 1/2" DIA. x 1 1/2" DOWEL

v 5/8" DIA. x 6" DOWEL
   DRILL END HOLES 1/2" DIA. x
   1/4" DEEP. DRILL CENTER HOLE
   1/2" DIA. x 1/4" DEEP AT 135°.

TO ASSURE PROPER FIT, DRILL
CENTER HOLE LAST AFTER ROD
IS INSTALLED IN "cc"

3/8"

2 5/8"

2 5/8"

3/8"

"A"

w 1/2" x 4 1/2" DOWEL
   2 - pcs

7/8"

DRILL 2 HOLES 1/2" DIA. 1/4" DEEP
AT 45°

3/8"

3/8"

45°

1 3/4"

2 3/16"

1/4"

SCALE:
3/8" = 1"
UNLESS NOTED

x 1/2" x 3 1/2" x 7"

y 3/4" x 3/4" x 3 1/2"

1/2"

z 1/2" x 1" x 7"

DRILL 11/16" DIA.
HOLE THRU

aa 3/8" DIA. FURNITURE PLUG

bb 1/2" DIA.
    FURNITURE PLUG.
    4 - pcs

cc CONTROL ROD
    SEE SECTION "A"

1/2"

1/2"

1/2"

1 1/2"

1/4"

1 1/2"

5/8"

1/4"

1 5/8"

1 1/4"

45°

1/2"

1 1/2"

3"

1 3/8"

DETAIL "A"
SCALE: 1/2"=1"

DUMP TRUCK
An old-fashioned wooden
dump truck that has a positive
dump action and a swivel-
opening tail gate with brass
latch. It's sized to work with
all the other construction toys.
Size: 19″ long, 8″ wide.

STEAM SHOVEL
A nice-sized toy to teach co-ordination. The right-side crank moves bucket up and down. The left-side crank moves bucket forward and backward. The cab swivels on its base, giving unlimited digging and dumping action. Has a simple and effective spring-loaded dump action. Size: 12" long, 17" high.

STRÖM PUZZLES
Oskar says:

The puzzling Ströms have been cut from wood;
And look intriguing, like they should.
All four puzzles are on one plan.
Put them together, if you can.

Paint pattern and color suggestions
included. For ages 5 or 6 to adult.

STAND-UP PUZZLES
Interlocking pieces of thick wood that
stand by themselves. Painted on both
sides, they are much harder to put
together than they look. Subject
animals polar bear, seal cubs, whale
and eagle are all on the endangered
species list. Size: For ages 7 or 8
to adult.

90

SAILFISH PUZZLE
A fun-to-do, two-dimensional puzzle
that children can play with after it's
put together.

BLOCK DOWEL PUZZLE
A simple pull-apart puzzle for young
children.

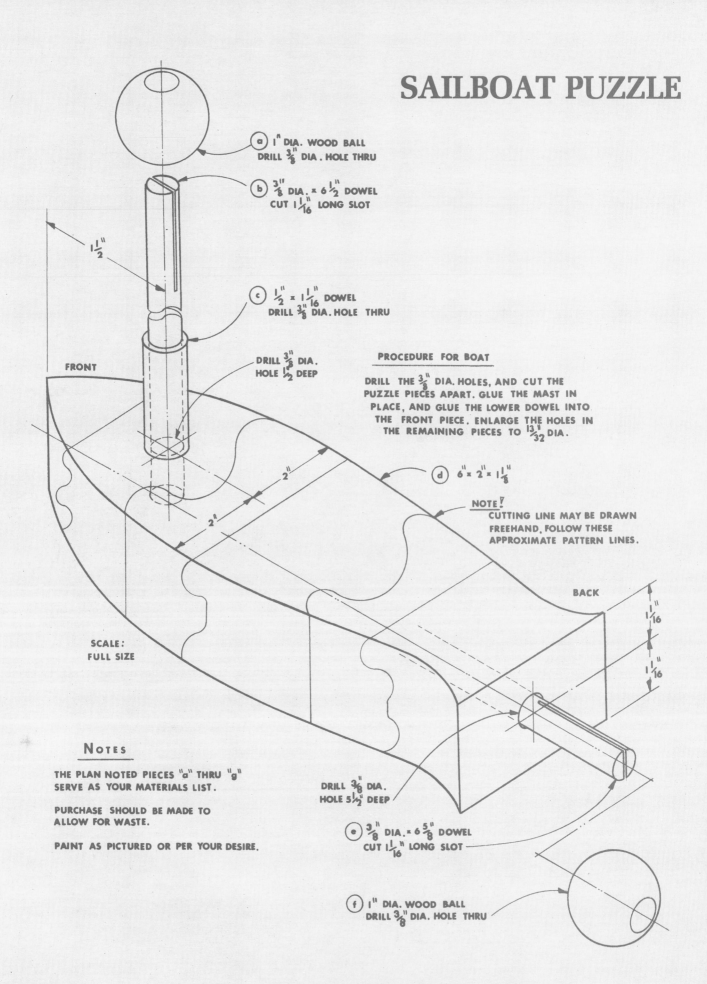

SAILBOAT PUZZLE

(a) 1" DIA. WOOD BALL
DRILL $\frac{3}{8}$" DIA. HOLE THRU

(b) $\frac{3}{8}$" DIA. × 6$\frac{1}{2}$" DOWEL
CUT 1$\frac{1}{16}$" LONG SLOT

(c) $\frac{1}{2}$" × 1$\frac{1}{16}$" DOWEL
DRILL $\frac{3}{8}$" DIA. HOLE THRU

1$\frac{1}{2}$"

FRONT

DRILL $\frac{3}{8}$" DIA.
HOLE 1$\frac{1}{2}$" DEEP

PROCEDURE FOR BOAT

DRILL THE $\frac{3}{8}$" DIA. HOLES, AND CUT THE
PUZZLE PIECES APART. GLUE THE MAST IN
PLACE, AND GLUE THE LOWER DOWEL INTO
THE FRONT PIECE. ENLARGE THE HOLES IN
THE REMAINING PIECES TO $\frac{13}{32}$" DIA.

2"

2"

(d) 6" × 2" × 1$\frac{1}{8}$"

NOTE!
CUTTING LINE MAY BE DRAWN
FREEHAND, FOLLOW THESE
APPROXIMATE PATTERN LINES.

BACK

1$\frac{1}{16}$"

1$\frac{1}{16}$"

SCALE:
FULL SIZE

NOTES

THE PLAN NOTED PIECES "a" THRU "g"
SERVE AS YOUR MATERIALS LIST.

PURCHASE SHOULD BE MADE TO
ALLOW FOR WASTE.

PAINT AS PICTURED OR PER YOUR DESIRE.

DRILL $\frac{3}{8}$" DIA.
HOLE 5$\frac{1}{2}$" DEEP

(e) $\frac{3}{8}$" DIA. × 6$\frac{5}{8}$" DOWEL
CUT 1$\frac{1}{16}$" LONG SLOT

(f) 1" DIA. WOOD BALL
DRILL $\frac{3}{8}$" DIA. HOLE THRU

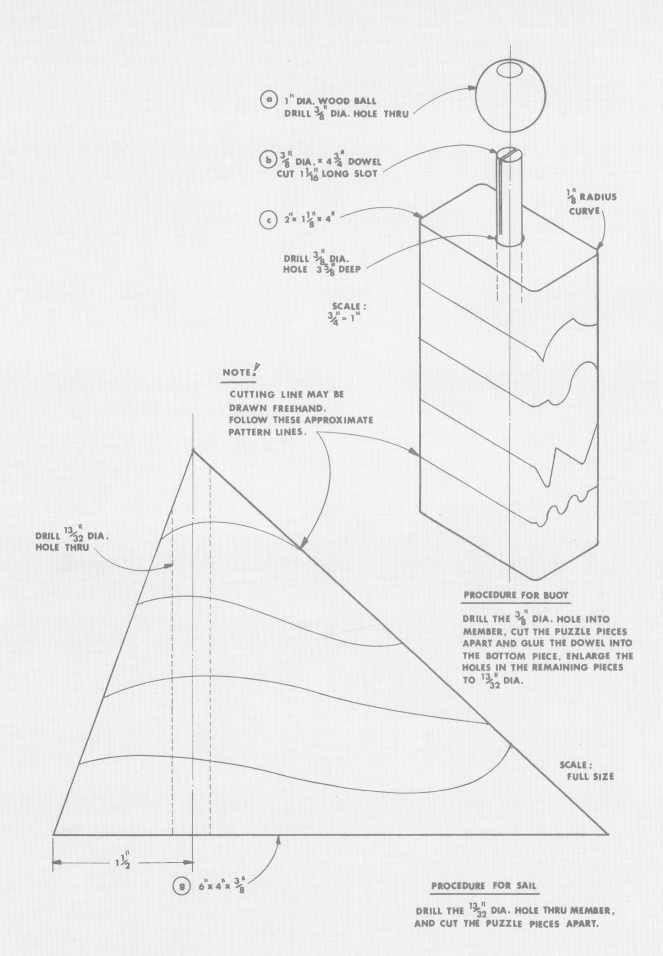

(a) 1" DIA. WOOD BALL
DRILL $\frac{3}{8}$" DIA. HOLE THRU

(b) $\frac{3}{8}$" DIA. × 4$\frac{3}{4}$" DOWEL
CUT 1$\frac{1}{16}$" LONG SLOT

(c) 2"× 1$\frac{1}{8}$"× 4"

DRILL $\frac{3}{8}$" DIA.
HOLE 3$\frac{5}{8}$" DEEP

$\frac{1}{8}$" RADIUS
CURVE

SCALE:
$\frac{3}{4}$" = 1"

NOTE!

CUTTING LINE MAY BE
DRAWN FREEHAND.
FOLLOW THESE APPROXIMATE
PATTERN LINES.

DRILL $\frac{13}{32}$" DIA.
HOLE THRU

1$\frac{1}{2}$"

(g) 6"× 4"× $\frac{3}{8}$"

PROCEDURE FOR BUOY

DRILL THE $\frac{3}{8}$" DIA. HOLE INTO
MEMBER, CUT THE PUZZLE PIECES
APART AND GLUE THE DOWEL INTO
THE BOTTOM PIECE. ENLARGE THE
HOLES IN THE REMAINING PIECES
TO $\frac{13}{32}$" DIA.

SCALE:
FULL SIZE

PROCEDURE FOR SAIL

DRILL THE $\frac{13}{32}$" DIA. HOLE THRU MEMBER,
AND CUT THE PUZZLE PIECES APART.

95

PRICE LIST FOR TOY PLANS

Page	Name	Price
58-59	**Entire Mystic Seaport**	$18.00
	Marina only—includes crane, dock, lighthouse, range markers, & channel markers. Plus plan for people.	$ 4.00
	Town—all buildings, plus plan for people	6.00
	Four sailboat plans—2-masted schooner, 3-masted schooner, small cabin sloop, small class racing boat.	3.00
	Three power boats—motor cruiser, fishing trawler, shrimp boat.	2.50
	Work boats—Tug boat, barge, cargo blocks and bags.	2.50
	Stern wheeler	3.50
	Side Wheeler—includes eagle pattern.	3.00
	Car Ferry	2.00
67	**Ferris Wheel**—includes patterns for people.	6.00
68	**Prancer**—plan includes full-size patterns for horse and rocker, leather stirrups and bridle, saddle, saddle cushion, and painted design on rocker. Mane and tail construction suggestions.	12.00
68	**Norse Steed**—plan includes full-size patterns for lower rocker section and horse's head, saddle, saddle cushion, bridle, and stencil designs, plus instructions for mane and tail.	12.00
69	**Tumbleweed**	4.00
72	**Bank**—includes Ström Vault painting pattern.	2.00
73	**Doll Buggy**—includes buggy liner pattern.	6.00
	Optional hardware package—Wood applique designs, 4 brass hinge parts, rubber tread for wheels.	4.50
73	**Ström Wagon**	7.50
	Option—rubber tread for wheels, 1.20 ea. wheel.	
74-75	**Front End Loader**—includes plan for people.	4.00
74-75	**Cement Mixer**—includes plan for people.	7.50
	Optional hardware package—2 springs, 2 gears, 4 ft. drive chain.	6.40

Page	Name	Price
78-79	**Boom Crane**—includes plan for people	6.00
	Optional hardware package—3 springs, 2 gears.	4.50
78-79	**Stake Truck & Trailer.** Includes barrel pattern and patterns for people.	6.00
80	**Sand Conveyor**	7.50
	Optional hardware package—7 gears, 1 spring, 13 ft. drive chain.	19.00
81	**Tow Truck**—includes plan for people.	5.00
	Optional hardware package—12″ brass jack chain, 1 spring.	1.20
82-83	**Bulldozer**—includes plan for people.	4.00
82-83	**Steamroller**—includes plan for people.	5.00
	Optional hardware package—1 chain drive, 2 gear, steering chain.	4.00
88-89	**Steam Shovel**—includes plan for people.	6.00
	Optional hardware package—4 springs	2.00
88-89	**Dump Truck**—includes plan for people.	5.00
90	**Ström Character Puzzles**—2 on 1 sheet Two women together on 1 sheet Oskar and Slug Hog on 1 sheet	3.00 a sheet
91	**Wildlife Puzzles**— 2 on 1 sheet Eagle and whale together—whale has pattern for painting. Bears and seals together, painting patterns included.	3.00 a sheet
92	**Sailboat and Simple Dowel Pull-Apart Puzzles** 2 on 1 sheet	2.00

All prices include postage and handling. We *prefer* to send UPS, whenever possible, so please include your street address.

SEND PLAN ORDERS TO:
SUN DESIGNS
P.O. Box 206
Delafield, WI 53018

Check, Money Order, MasterCard, or VISA with order. Please include account number and expiration date with charge orders. Wisconsin residents *only* add 5% sales tax.